Getting Started with C++ Audio Programming for Game Development

A hands-on guide to audio programming in game development with the FMOD audio library and toolkit

David Gouveia

PUBLISHING

BIRMINGHAM - MUMBAI

Getting Started with C++ Audio Programming for Game Development

First published: August, 2013

Production Reference: 1190813

Published by Packt Publishing Ltd.
Livery Place
35 Livery Street
Birmingham B3 2PB, UK.

ISBN 978-1-84969-909-9

www.packtpub.com

Cover Image by Suresh Mogre (suresh.mogre.99@gmail.com)

Credits

Author
David Gouveia

Reviewers
Tomas Pettersson
Daniel Varela

Acquisition Editor
Edward Gordon

Commissioning Editor
Shreerang Deshpande

Technical Editors
Larissa Pinto
Nitee Shetty

Project Coordinator
Suraj Bist

Proofreader
Lesley Harrison

Indexer
Tejal Soni

Graphics
Abhinash Sahu

Production Coordinator
Melwyn D'sa

Cover Work
Melwyn D'sa

About the Author

David Gouveia is a Software Engineer and Game Developer from Portugal, Madeira Island. He recently finished his MSc in Computer Science, with a specialization in graphics and multimedia, and is currently working full-time as a game programmer for a local company. He runs an educational blog about game development and enjoys sharing his knowledge with the community whenever possible. His main interests in game development are graphics and audio programming. He also has a strong interest in music and synthesizers, having played the keyboard most of his life.

About the Reviewers

Tomas Pettersson is a creator of the freeware audio tools SFXR and Musagi.

Daniel Varela was born in Trebujena, Spain, in 1980. His strong passion for music and technology led him to obtain a Bachelor's degree in Sound and Image Engineering from the University of Málaga, Spain, in 2004.

From very early on in his education, he focused on digital audio signal processing, designing and developing software simulations for audio signals quantification noise modeling, experimental reverb effects, and culminating in an application for the digital audio editing as his final project of studies.

After graduating, he worked for six years in the software consultancy area as an Applications Programmer and Analyst. During this stage, he improved his Object Oriented Programming skills and working methodology, but however, he felt like something was missing.

In 2010, he joined TheGameKitchen, a just born indie videogames development company, as a Generalist Programmer. During this period, he made familiar game engines, such as XNA or Unity3D and developed some audio application prototypes, such as a MOD tracker player for XNA or a scratching application for Windows Phone.

In 2011, he started working at BlitzGamesStudios in the UK as Audio Programmer, developing a successful career in the area of audio programming for videogames. He is responsible for maintaining and improving an existing cross platform end to end audio pipeline, as well as working with third party audio middleware such as FMOD and Wwise.

www.PacktPub.com

Support files, eBooks, discount offers and more

You might want to visit www.PacktPub.com for support files and downloads related to your book.

Did you know that Packt offers eBook versions of every book published, with PDF and ePub files available? You can upgrade to the eBook version at www.PacktPub.com and as a print book customer, you are entitled to a discount on the eBook copy. Get in touch with us at service@packtpub.com for more details.

At www.PacktPub.com, you can also read a collection of free technical articles, sign up for a range of free newsletters and receive exclusive discounts and offers on Packt books and eBooks.

http://PacktLib.PacktPub.com

Do you need instant solutions to your IT questions? PacktLib is Packt's online digital book library. Here, you can access, read and search across Packt's entire library of books.

Why Subscribe?

- Fully searchable across every book published by Packt
- Copy and paste, print and bookmark content
- On demand and accessible via web browser

Free Access for Packt account holders

If you have an account with Packt at www.PacktPub.com, you can use this to access PacktLib today and view nine entirely free books. Simply use your login credentials for immediate access.

Table of Contents

Preface

Audio is certainly one of the most powerful tools at our disposal when it comes to making the players feel something from a video game. Audio can serve many different purposes in video games, such as giving feedback with sound effects, increasing immersion with ambient tracks, telling stories with recorded speech, or conveying all kinds of emotions through background music.

Video games have been making use of sound since their earliest days. For instance, the 1972 classic, Pong, used a beep sound effect to provide feedback whenever the ball collided with something, with different pitches used to distinguish between collisions with the walls, collisions with the paddles, or the ball leaving the game court.

Space Invaders, on the other hand, made a very clever use of its rudimentary background music by progressively increasing the speed of the song as the danger of the alien invasion drew closer, thus enhancing the feelings of tension within the player. Studies have shown that gamers that played the game without sound did not feel the same sense of urgency, and their heart rates did not rise like the ones that played the game with the sound turned on.

Since those days, there have been many advances in technology, which allowed audio in games to evolve considerably. Most games began using recorded audio instead of crude synthesized tones, and new techniques such as 3D audio now allow the players to feel like the sound is coming from all around them and interacting with the game environment.

Music has also played a very important role in video games. The popular Final Fantasy games owe a great portion of their emotional impact to the sweeping, cinematic soundtracks composed by Nobuo Uematsu. The most memorable scenes in the series would have not been the same without the music that accompanied them.

Many developers and composers have also looked into ways of making the music react to the game play. For example, starting with *Monkey Island 2*, *LeChuck's Revenge*, every graphic adventure game that LucasArts created uses a custom interactive music system called iMUSE, which among other features, allows seamless musical transitions between themes as the player moves from one room to another.

There are even games that incorporate audio concepts directly into their main gameplay mechanics, such as the songs that the player has to memorize and play in *The Legend of Zelda: Ocarina of Time*, and games that revolve entirely around sound, with the most popular examples being rhythm games, such as *PaRappa the Rapper*, *Dance Dance Revolution*, or *Guitar Hero*.

However, despite being such an important part of video games, many game development books skim through the subject of audio programming. Even the ones that dedicate a chapter to audio, often only teach you the very basics, such as loading and playing audio files, or use outdated audio engines instead of the ones used by the industry nowadays. Additionally, other game development topics, such as graphics, physics, or artificial intelligence tend to be more enticing to beginner level game developers and learning about audio becomes less of a priority.

The main goal of this book is to give you a crash course on audio programming for games by using a popular and well-established audio engine, and covering the subject from several different levels of abstraction. It is my hope that this approach will give you enough knowledge to implement most of the audio features that are normally required for a video game, and form a foundation so that you may pursue other topics that are more advanced.

What this book covers

Chapter 1, *Audio Concepts*, covers some of the most important audio concepts, such as sound waves, analog and digital audio, multi-channel audio, and audio file formats.

Chapter 2, *Audio Playback*, shows how to use FMOD to load and play audio files, and how to begin creating a simple audio manager class.

Chapter 3, *Audio Control*, shows how to control the playback and parameters of a sound, and how to group sounds into categories and control them simultaneously.

Chapter 4, *3D Audio*, covers the most important concepts of 3D audio, such as positional audio, reverberation, obstruction/occlusion, along with a few DSP effects.

Chapter 5, *Intelligent Audio*, provides an overview of high-level sound design using the FMOD Designer tool, with examples of how to create adaptive and interactive sound events and music.

Chapter 6, Low-level Audio, provides basic information on how to work with audio at a very low-level, by manipulating and writing audio data directly.

What you need for this book

For this book, you will need the following software:

- **C++ IDE**: Instructions are provided for Microsoft Visual Studio, but you should be able to use any C++ IDE or compiler. The Express version of Visual Studio is free and can be downloaded from the Microsoft website.

- **FMOD Ex**: Needed for chapters 2 - 4, and 6 and can be downloaded for free from `www.fmod.org`.

- **FMOD Designer**: Needed for chapter 5. Can be downloaded for free from `www.fmod.org`.

- **SFML**: All of the code samples on the website also use SFML (Version 2.0) to handle other tasks, such as window management, graphics, and input handling. Free download from `www.sfml-dev.org`.

Who this book is for

This book is oriented towards C++ game developers who have little or no experience with audio programming and would like a quick introduction to the most important topics required to integrate audio into a game.

You will need an intermediate knowledge of C++ to be able to follow the code examples in the book, including an understanding of basic C++ Standard Library features, such as strings, containers, iterators, and streams. Some game programming experience is also recommended, but not mandatory.

Conventions

In this book, you will find a number of styles of text that distinguish between different kinds of information. Here are some examples of these styles, and an explanation of their meaning.

Code words in text, database table names, folder names, filenames, file extensions, pathnames, dummy URLs, user input, and Twitter handles are shown as follows: "Notice that the function returns the `system` object through a parameter."

A block of code is set as follows:

```
#include <math.h>

float ChangeOctave(float frequency, float variation) {
  static float octave_ratio = 2.0f;
  return frequency * pow(octave_ratio, variation);
}
float ChangeSemitone(float frequency, float variation) {
  static float semitone_ratio = pow(2.0f, 1.0f / 12.0f);
  return frequency * pow(semitone_ratio, variation);
}
```

When we wish to draw your attention to a particular part of a code block, the relevant lines or items are set in bold:

```
#include <SFML/Window.hpp>
#include "SimpleAudioManager.h"

int main() {
  sf::Window window(sf::VideoMode(320, 240), "AudioPlayback");
  sf::Clock clock;

  // Place your initialization logic here
  SimpleAudioManager audio;
  audio.Load("explosion.wav");

  // Start the game loop
  while (window.isOpen()) {
    // Only run approx 60 times per second
    float elapsed = clock.getElapsedTime().asSeconds();
    if (elapsed < 1.0f / 60.0f) continue;
    clock.restart();
    sf::Event event;
    while (window.pollEvent(event)) {
      // Handle window events
      if (event.type == sf::Event::Closed)
        window.close();

      // Handle user input
      if (event.type == sf::Event::KeyPressed &&
          event.key.code == sf::Keyboard::Space)
        audio.Play("explosion.wav");
    }
    // Place your update and draw logic here
```

```
    audio.Update(elapsed);
  }
  // Place your shutdown logic here
  return 0;
}
```

New terms and **important words** are shown in bold. Words that you see on the screen, in menus or dialog boxes for example, appear in the text like this: "For all the steps that follow, make sure that the **Configuration** option is set to **All Configurations**."

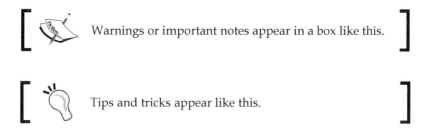

Warnings or important notes appear in a box like this.

Tips and tricks appear like this.

Reader feedback

Feedback from our readers is always welcome. Let us know what you think about this book—what you liked or may have disliked. Reader feedback is important for us to develop titles that you really get the most out of.

To send us general feedback, simply send an e-mail to feedback@packtpub.com, and mention the book title via the subject of your message.

If there is a topic that you have expertise in and you are interested in either writing or contributing to a book, see our author guide on www.packtpub.com/authors.

Customer support

Now that you are the proud owner of a Packt book, we have a number of things to help you to get the most from your purchase.

Downloading the example code

You can download the example code files for all Packt books you have purchased from your account at http://www.packtpub.com. If you purchased this book elsewhere, you can visit http://www.packtpub.com/support and register to have the files e-mailed directly to you.

Errata

Although we have taken every care to ensure the accuracy of our content, mistakes do happen. If you find a mistake in one of our books—maybe a mistake in the text or the code—we would be grateful if you would report this to us. By doing so, you can save other readers from frustration and help us improve subsequent versions of this book. If you find any errata, please report them by visiting http://www.packtpub.com/submit-errata, selecting your book, clicking on the **errata submission form** link, and entering the details of your errata. Once your errata are verified, your submission will be accepted and the errata will be uploaded on our website, or added to any list of existing errata, under the Errata section of that title. Any existing errata can be viewed by selecting your title from http://www.packtpub.com/support.

Piracy

Piracy of copyright material on the Internet is an ongoing problem across all media. At Packt, we take the protection of our copyright and licenses very seriously. If you come across any illegal copies of our works, in any form, on the Internet, please provide us with the location address or website name immediately so that we can pursue a remedy.

Please contact us at copyright@packtpub.com with a link to the suspected pirated material.

We appreciate your help in protecting our authors, and our ability to bring you valuable content.

Questions

You can contact us at questions@packtpub.com if you are having a problem with any aspect of the book, and we will do our best to address it.

1
Audio Concepts

Programming the audio component of a game is a lot easier these days, thanks to all the powerful audio libraries that are available. These libraries ease the burden on the developers by taking care of most of the low-level implementation details. While this is a good thing, it also makes it easier to dismiss the need to understand sound theory. For instance, we can easily play a sound file without knowing anything about its representation in memory.

However, even when we are using an audio library, there are still situations that will require some theoretical knowledge. For instance, we will often find parameters and function names related to the theory, such as the frequency of a sound, or the bit depth of an audio buffer. Knowing the meaning of these concepts is important to ensure that we are using them properly.

The goal of this chapter is to serve as a light introduction to the concepts that we will need the most during the course of this book.

Sound waves

Sound is created from the vibrations of objects. These vibrations produce variations in the atmospheric pressure which propagate away from the objects in the form of sound waves. Our ears are capable of detecting incoming sound waves and converting them into nerve signals that our brain interprets as sound.

One way to visualize sound is to draw a graph of the variations in the atmospheric pressure at each moment in time. However, understanding how those graphs relate to what we hear can be extremely complex. For that reason, we usually start by studying the simplest type of wave, the **sine wave**.

The sine wave is interesting for educational purposes, because we can easily identify two of the main properties of sound from it: volume and pitch. Most audio libraries allow us to control both of these properties for any sounds that we play.

- **Volume**: This property corresponds to how loud or quiet the sound is. It depends directly on the amplitude (or the height) of the sound wave, as measured on the vertical axis. The main unit of volume is the decibel (dB), but most audio libraries use a scale between zero (silence) and one (full volume).

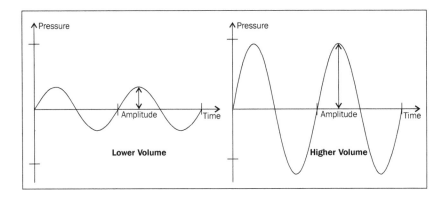

- **Pitch**: This property determines how high or low the sound is. It depends on the frequency of the sound wave, which is the number of times that it repeats every second. The unit of frequency is the hertz (Hz). Two things that you should know about frequency are that the human ear can only hear frequencies within the 20 Hz and 20,000 Hz range, and that most sounds that you hear are actually a combination of several different frequencies.

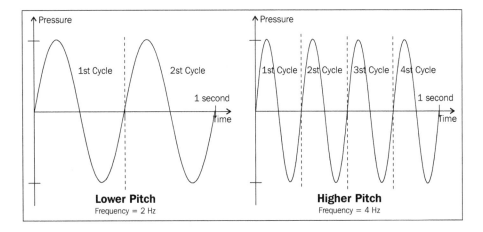

Analog and digital audio

Now that we know what sound is, let us turn our thoughts towards recording the sound and storing it on a computer. The first step in this process is to convert the sound wave into an electrical signal. When we use a continuous signal to represent another signal of a different quantity, we call it an **analog signal** or in the case of a sound wave, an **analog audio signal**. You are probably already familiar with the devices that perform this conversion:

- **Microphones**: These are devices that convert sound waves into electrical signals
- **Speakers**: These are devices that convert electrical signals into sound waves

Analog signals have many uses, but most computers cannot work with them directly. Computers can only operate on sequences of discrete binary numbers, also known as **digital signals**. We need to convert the analog signal recorded by the microphone into a digital signal, that is, digital audio, before the computer can understand it.

The most common method used to represent analog signals digitally is **pulse code modulation (PCM)**. The general idea of PCM is to sample (or measure) the amplitude of the analog signal at fixed time intervals, and store the results as an array of numbers (called samples). Since the original data is continuous, and numbers on a computer are discrete, samples need to be rounded to the nearest available number, in a process known as **quantization**. Samples are usually stored as integer numbers, but it is also possible to use floating-point numbers as shown in the following example:

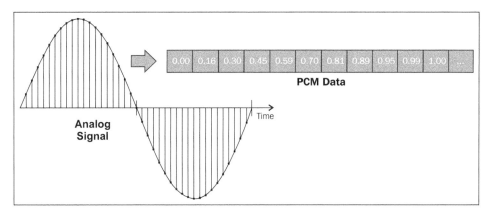

There are two ways to control the quality of the sampled audio:

- **Sampling rate**: Also known as the sampling frequency, it is the amount of samples taken for each second of audio. According to the Nyquist sampling theorem, the sampling rate should be at least twice as high as the highest frequency of the analog signal, in order to allow a proper reconstruction. You will usually work with values of 44,100 Hz or 48,000 Hz. The following figure compares sampling at different rates:

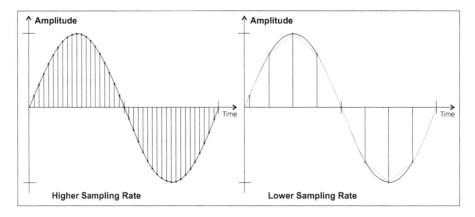

- **Bit depth**: Also known as the resolution, it is the amount of bits used to represent a single sample. This controls the number of possible discrete values that each sample can take, and needs to be high enough to avoid quantization errors. You will usually work with bit depths of 16 bits or 24 bits, stored as integer numbers, or 32 bits stored as floating-point numbers. The following figure compares sampling at different resolutions:

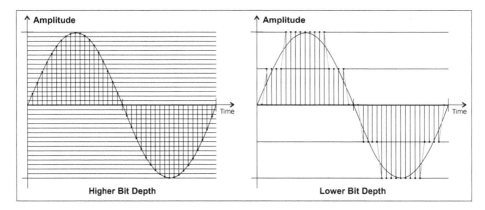

Multi-channel audio

Another aspect that we should talk about is that many audio systems have more than one output. By sending different audio signals to separate outputs (called channels), it is possible to produce the illusion of directionality and space. The number of channels on these systems can vary from one (**mono**) or two (**stereo**), to several more on surround sound systems.

The PCM format described earlier can store audio for multiple channels at once, by interleaving one sample from each channel in the correct order. The following figure shows an example of this for a stereo system:

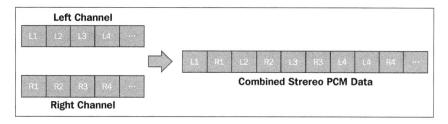

Besides volume and pitch, which we have examined earlier, there is another property that you will usually find in every audio library, called **panning**. Panning applies to stereo systems, and allows you to simulate the position of the sound, placing it anywhere between the left and the right channels. For positioning in configurations with more than two channels, you normally use other advanced features, such as 3D sound.

Audio file formats

There are so many different file formats for storing audio on a computer that it is easy to feel overwhelmed at first. Thankfully, you will only use a couple of them in your games, most of the time. Audio file formats usually fall into one of the following categories:

- **Uncompressed audio files**: These are audio files where the data is stored in its original state (normally PCM). This means that their data is already prepared for playback without any further processing. The downside is that they take up a lot of space on disc (approximately 10 MB for one minute of audio). For example, WAV and AIFF.

- **Lossless compression**: These are audio files where the data is encoded using compression algorithms that only perform reversible changes, so that no information is permanently lost. These files can be up to half the size of the uncompressed formats, but need the computer to decode them before playback. For example, FLAC and APE.

- **Lossy compression**: These are the audio files where the data is encoded using compression algorithms where some loss of the information is acceptable. These algorithms use heuristics to determine which parts of the data are less likely to be audible, in order to discard them. File sizes can be as small as 10 percent of the original size, although sound quality can suffer considerably if the compression is too strong. For example, MP3, WMA, and OGG.

- **Sequenced music**: There are some formats that do not fit into any of the earlier mentioned categories. For example, MIDI files only store information about how the music should be played, but do not contain any sound data, leaving it to the computers to decide how they should be interpreted. For this reason, they are extremely small, but sound quality is limited, and varies from system to system. There are also hybrid formats such as MOD files (also known as module or tracker files), which are in many ways similar to MIDI files, but also contain any sound data that is required to play them (known as instruments).

Be aware that despite its popularity, the MP3 is a patented format, and you cannot use it commercially without paying royalties (refer to `http://mp3licensing.com/` for more information). For this book, we will be using OGG files for long sounds, and WAV files for small sound effects.

Summary

In this chapter, we have seen that sound is a series of variations in atmospheric pressure, travelling in the form of sound waves. We also saw that sound waves have properties such as amplitude and frequency, which control how loud or high it is and that you can represent a sound wave using electrical signals (analog audio) and a series of numbers (digital audio). We learned that when converting an analog signal to a digital signal, you need to control the sampling rate and the bit depth. Finally, we saw that many audio systems have more than one output and that there are many different types of audio file formats.

2
Audio Playback

In this chapter, we will perform two of the most fundamental operations in audio programming—loading and playing audio files. This might not seem like much, but it is already enough to get us started adding audio into our games.

There are many different audio libraries available these days, such as DirectSound, Core Audio, PortAudio, OpenAL, FMOD, or Wwise. Some are available only on certain platforms, while others work almost everywhere. Some are very low-level, providing little more than a bridge between the user and the sound card driver, while others provide high-level features such as 3D sound or interactive music.

For this book, we will be using FMOD, a cross-platform audio middleware developed by Firelight Technologies that is extremely powerful, yet easy-to-use. However, you should try to focus more on the concepts covered, instead of the API, because understanding them will allow you to adapt to other libraries more easily, since a lot of this knowledge is interchangeable.

For starters, we will learn how to install FMOD, how to initialize and update the audio system, and how to get it to play an audio file. At the end of the chapter, we will work through the creation of a very simple audio manager class, which encapsulates all of these tasks behind a minimalistic interface.

Understanding FMOD

One of the main reasons why I chose FMOD for this book is that it contains two separate APIs—the FMOD Ex Programmer's API, for low-level audio playback, and FMOD Designer, for high-level data-driven audio. This will allow us to cover game audio programming at different levels of abstraction without having to use entirely different technologies.

Downloading the example code

You can download the example code files for all Packt books you have purchased from your account at http://www.packtpub.com. If you purchased this book elsewhere, you can visit http://www.packtpub.com/support and register to have the files e-mailed directly to you.

Besides that reason, FMOD is also an excellent piece of software, with several advantages to game developers:

- **License**: It is free for non-commercial use, and has reasonable licenses for commercial projects.
- **Cross-platform**: It works across an impressive number of platforms. You can run it on Windows, Mac, Linux, Android, iOS, and on most of the modern video game consoles by Sony, Microsoft, and Nintendo.
- **Supported formats**: It has native support for a huge range of audio file formats, which saves you the trouble of having to include other external libraries and decoders.
- **Programming languages**: Not only can you use FMOD with C and C++, there are also bindings available for other programming languages, such as C# and Python.
- **Popularity**: It is extremely popular, being widely considered as the industry standard nowadays. It was used in games such as BioShock, Crysis, Diablo 3, Guitar Hero, Start Craft II, and World of Warcraft. It is also used to power several popular game engines, such as Unity3D and CryEngine.
- **Features**: It is packed with features, covering everything from simple audio playback, streaming and 3D sound, to interactive music, DSP effects and low-level audio programming.

Installing FMOD Ex Programmer's API

Installing a C++ library can be a bit daunting at first. The good side is that once you have done it for the first time, the process is usually the same for every other library. Here are the steps that you should follow if you are using Microsoft Visual Studio:

1. Download the FMOD Ex Programmer's API from http://www.fmod.org and install it to a folder that you can remember, such as C:\FMOD.

2. Create a new empty project, and add at least one .cpp file to it. Then, right-click on the project node on the **Solution Explorer**, and select **Properties** from the list. For all the steps that follow, make sure that the **Configuration** option is set to **All Configurations**.

3. Navigate to **C/C++ | General**, and add `C:\FMOD\api\inc` to the list of **Additional Include Directories** (entries are separated by semicolons).

4. Navigate to **Linker | General**, and add `C:\FMOD\api\lib` to the list of **Additional Library Directories**.

5. Navigate to **Linker | Input**, and add `fmodex_vc.lib` to the list of **Additional Dependencies**.

6. Navigate to **Build Events | Post-Build Event**, and add `xcopy /y "C:\FMOD\api\fmodex.dll" "$(OutDir)"` to the **Command Line** list.

7. Include the `<fmod.hpp>` header file from your code.

Creating and managing the audio system

Everything that happens inside FMOD is managed by a class named `FMOD::System`, which we must start by instantiating with the `FMOD::System_Create()` function:

```
FMOD::System* system;
FMOD::System_Create(&system);
```

Notice that the function returns the `system` object through a parameter. You will see this pattern every time one of the FMOD functions needs to return a value, because they all reserve the regular return value for an error code. We will discuss error checking in a bit, but for now let us get the audio engine up and running.

Now that we have a `system` object instantiated, we also need to initialize it by calling the `init()` method:

```
system->init(100, FMOD_INIT_NORMAL, 0);
```

The first parameter specifies the maximum number of channels to allocate. This controls how many sounds you are able to play simultaneously. You can choose any number for this parameter because the system performs some clever priority management behind the scenes and distributes the channels using the available resources. The second and third parameters customize the initialization process, and you can usually leave them as shown in the example.

Many features that we will use work properly only if we update the `system` object every frame. This is done by calling the `update()` method from inside your game loop:

```
system->update();
```

You should also remember to shutdown the `system` object before your game ends, so that it can dispose of all resources. This is done by calling the `release()` method:

```
system->release();
```

Loading and streaming audio files

One of the greatest things about FMOD is that you can load virtually any audio file format with a single method call. To load an audio file into memory, use the createSound() method:

```
FMOD::Sound* sound;
system->createSound("sfx.wav", FMOD_DEFAULT, 0, &sound);
```

To stream an audio file from disk without having to store it in memory, use the createStream() method:

```
FMOD::Sound* stream;
system->createStream("song.ogg", FMOD_DEFAULT, 0, &stream);
```

Both methods take the path of the audio file as the first parameter, and return a pointer to an FMOD::Sound object through the fourth parameter, which you can use to play the sound. The paths in the previous examples are relative to the application path. If you are running these examples in Visual Studio, make sure that you copy the audio files into the output folder (for example, using a post-build event such as xcopy /y "$(ProjectDir)*.ogg" "$(OutDir)").

The choice between loading and streaming is mostly a tradeoff between memory and processing power. When you load an audio file, all of its data is uncompressed and stored in memory, which can take up a lot of space, but the computer can play it without much effort. Streaming, on the other hand, barely uses any memory, but the computer has to access the disk constantly, and decode the audio data on the fly. Another difference (in FMOD at least) is that when you stream a sound, you can only have one instance of it playing at any time. This limitation exists because there is only one decode buffer per stream. Therefore, for sound effects that have to be played multiple times simultaneously, you have to either load them into memory, or open multiple concurrent streams. As a rule of thumb, streaming is great for music tracks, voice cues, and ambient tracks, while most sound effects should be loaded into memory.

The second and third parameters allow us to customize the behavior of the sound. There are many different options available, but the following list summarizes the ones we will be using the most. Using FMOD_DEFAULT is equivalent to combining the first option of each of these categories:

- FMOD_LOOP_OFF and FMOD_LOOP_NORMAL: These modes control whether the sound should only play once, or loop once it reaches the end

- FMOD_HARDWARE and FMOD_SOFTWARE: These modes control whether the sound should be mixed in hardware (better performance) or software (more features)

- FMOD_2D and FMOD_3D: These modes control whether to use 3D sound

We can combine multiple modes using the bitwise OR operator (for instance, FMOD_DEFAULT | FMOD_LOOP_NORMAL | FMOD_SOFTWARE). We can also tell the system to stream a sound even when we are using the createSound() method, by setting the FMOD_CREATESTREAM flag. In fact, the createStream() method is simply a shortcut for this.

When we do not need a sound anymore (or at the end of the game) we should dispose of it by calling the release() method of the sound object. We should always release the sounds we create, regardless of the audio system also being released.

```
sound->release();
```

Playing sounds

With the sounds loaded into memory or prepared for streaming, all that is left is telling the system to play them using the playSound() method:

```
FMOD::Channel* channel;
system->playSound(FMOD_CHANNEL_FREE, sound, false, &channel);
```

The first parameter selects in which channel the sound will play. You should usually let FMOD handle it automatically, by passing FMOD_CHANNEL_FREE as the parameter.

The second parameter is a pointer to the FMOD::Sound object that you want to play.

The third parameter controls whether the sound should start in a paused state, giving you a chance to modify some of its properties without the changes being audible. If you set this to true, you will also need to use the next parameter so that you can unpause it later.

The fourth parameter is an output parameter that returns a pointer to the FMOD::Channel object in which the sound will play. You can use this handle to control the sound in multiple ways, which will be the main topic of the next chapter.

You can ignore this last parameter if you do not need any control over the sound, and simply pass in 0 in its place. This can be useful for non-lopping one-shot sounds.

```
system->playSound(FMOD_CHANNEL_FREE, sound, false, 0);
```

Checking for errors

So far, we have assumed that every operation will always work without errors. However, in a real scenario, there is room for a lot to go wrong. For example, we could try to load an audio file that does not exist.

In order to report errors, every function and method in FMOD has a return value of type FMOD_RESULT, which will only be equal to FMOD_OK if everything went right. It is up to the user to check this value and react accordingly:

```
FMOD_RESULT result = system->init(100, FMOD_INIT_NORMAL, 0);
if (result != FMOD_OK) {
  // There was an error, do something about it
}
```

For starters, it would be useful to know what the error was. However, since FMOD_RESULT is an enumeration, you will only see a number if you try to print it. Fortunately, there is a function called FMOD_ErrorString() inside the fmod_errors.h header file which will give you a complete description of the error.

You might also want to create a helper function to simplify the error checking process. For instance, the following function will check for errors, print a description of the error to the standard output, and exit the application:

```
#include <iostream>
#include <fmod_errors.h>

void ExitOnError(FMOD_RESULT result) {
  if (result != FMOD_OK) {
    std::cout << FMOD_ErrorString(result) << std::endl;
    exit(-1);
  }
}
```

You could then use that function to check for any critical errors that should cause the application to abort:

```
ExitOnError(system->init(100, FMOD_INIT_NORMAL, 0));
```

The initialization process described earlier also assumes that everything will go as planned, but a real game should be prepared to deal with any errors. Fortunately, there is a template provided in the FMOD documentation which shows you how to write a robust initialization sequence. It is a bit long to cover here, so I urge you to refer to the file named Getting started with FMOD for Windows.pdf inside the documentation folder for more information.

For clarity, all of the code examples will continue to be presented without error checking, but you should always check for errors in a real project.

Project 1 – building a simple audio manager

In this project, we will be creating a `SimpleAudioManager` class that combines everything that was covered in this chapter. Creating a wrapper for an underlying system that only exposes the operations that we need is known as the **façade design pattern**, and is very useful in order to keep things nice and simple.

Since we have not seen how to manipulate sound yet, do not expect this class to be powerful enough to be used in a complex game. Its main purpose will be to let you load and play one-shot sound effects with very little code (which could in fact be enough for very simple games).

It will also free you from the responsibility of dealing with sound objects directly (and having to release them) by allowing you to refer to any loaded sound by its filename. The following is an example of how to use the class:

```
SimpleAudioManager audio;
audio.Load("explosion.wav");
audio.Play("explosion.wav");
```

From an educational point of view, what is perhaps even more important is that you use this exercise as a way to get some ideas on how to adapt the technology to your needs. It will also form the basis of the next chapters in the book, where we will build systems that are more complex.

Class definition

Let us start by examining the class definition:

```
#include <string>
#include <map>
#include <fmod.hpp>

typedef std::map<std::string, FMOD::Sound*> SoundMap;

class SimpleAudioManager {
 public:
  SimpleAudioManager();
  ~SimpleAudioManager();
```

```
  void Update(float elapsed);
  void Load(const std::string& path);
  void Stream(const std::string& path);
  void Play(const std::string& path);
 private:
  void LoadOrStream(const std::string& path, bool stream);
  FMOD::System* system;
  SoundMap sounds;
};
```

From browsing through the list of public class members, it should be easy to deduce what it is capable of doing:

- The class can load audio files (given a path) using the `Load()` method

- The class can stream audio files (given a path) using the `Stream()` method

- The class can play audio files (given a path) using the `Play()` method (granted that they have been previously loaded or streamed)

- There is also an `Update()` method and a constructor/destructor pair to manage the sound system

The private class members, on the other hand, can tell us a lot about the inner workings of the class:

- At the core of the class is an instance of `FMOD::System` responsible for driving the entire sound engine. The class initializes the sound system on the constructor, and releases it on the destructor.

- Sounds are stored inside an associative container, which allows us to search for a sound given its file path. For this purpose, we will be relying on one of the C++ **Standard Template Library** (**STL**) associative containers, the `std::map` class, as well as the `std::string` class for storing the keys. Looking up a string key is a bit inefficient (compared to an integer, for example), but it should be fast enough for our needs. An advantage of having all the sounds stored on a single container is that we can easily iterate over them and release them from the class destructor.

- Since the code for loading and streaming audio file is almost the same, the common functionality has been extracted into a private method called `LoadOrStream()`, to which `Load()` and `Stream()` delegate all of the work. This prevents us from repeating the code needlessly.

Initialization and destruction

Now, let us walk through the implementation of each of these methods. First we have the class constructor, which is extremely simple, as the only thing that it needs to do is initialize the `system` object.

```
SimpleAudioManager::SimpleAudioManager() {
  FMOD::System_Create(&system);
  system->init(100, FMOD_INIT_NORMAL, 0);
}
```

Updating is even simpler, consisting of a single method call:

```
void SimpleAudioManager::Update(float elapsed) {
  system->update();
}
```

The destructor, on the other hand, needs to take care of releasing the `system` object, as well as all the sound objects that were created. This process is not that complicated though. First, we iterate over the map of sounds, releasing each one in turn, and clearing the map at the end. The syntax might seem a bit strange if you have never used an STL iterator before, but all that it means is to start at the beginning of the container, and keep advancing until we reach its end. Then we finish off by releasing the `system` object as usual.

```
SimpleAudioManager::~SimpleAudioManager() {
  // Release every sound object and clear the map
  SoundMap::iterator iter;
  for (iter = sounds.begin(); iter != sounds.end(); ++iter)
    iter->second->release();
  sounds.clear();

  // Release the system object
  system->release();
  system = 0;
}
```

Loading or streaming sounds

Next in line are the `Load()` and `Stream()` methods, but let us examine the private `LoadOrStream()` method first. This method takes the path of the audio file as a parameter, and checks if it has already been loaded (by querying the sound map). If the sound has already been loaded there is no need to do it again, so the method returns. Otherwise, the file is loaded (or streamed, depending on the value of the second parameter) and stored in the sound map under the appropriate key.

```
void SimpleAudioManager::LoadOrStream(const std::string& path, bool
stream) {
  // Ignore call if sound is already loaded
  if (sounds.find(path) != sounds.end()) return;

  // Load (or stream) file into a sound object
  FMOD::Sound* sound;
  if (stream)
    system->createStream(path.c_str(), FMOD_DEFAULT, 0, &sound);
  else
    system->createSound(path.c_str(), FMOD_DEFAULT, 0, &sound);

  // Store the sound object in the map using the path as key
  sounds.insert(std::make_pair(path, sound));
}
```

With the previous method in place, both the `Load()` and the `Stream()` methods can be trivially implemented as follows:

```
void SimpleAudioManager::Load(const std::string& path) {
  LoadOrStream(path, false);
}
void SimpleAudioManager::Stream(const std::string& path) {
  LoadOrStream(path, true);
}
```

Playing sounds

Finally, there is the `Play()` method, which works the other way around. It starts by checking if the sound has already been loaded, and does nothing if the sound is not found on the map. Otherwise, the sound is played using the default parameters.

```
void SimpleAudioManager::Play(const std::string& path) {
  // Search for a matching sound in the map
  SoundMap::iterator sound = sounds.find(path);
```

```
  // Ignore call if no sound was found
  if (sound == sounds.end()) return;

  // Otherwise play the sound
  system->playSound(FMOD_CHANNEL_FREE, sound->second, false, 0);
}
```

We could have tried to automatically load the sound in the case when it was not found. In general, this is not a good idea, because loading a sound is a costly operation, and we do not want that happening during a critical gameplay section where it could slow the game down. Instead, we should stick to having separate load and play operations.

A note about the code samples

Although this is a book about audio, all the samples need an environment to run on. In order to keep the audio portion of the samples as clear as possible, we will also be using the **Simple and Fast Multimedia Library 2.0 (SFML)** (http://www.sfml-dev.org). This library can very easily take care of all the miscellaneous tasks, such as window creation, timing, graphics, and user input, which you will find in any game.

For example, here is a complete sample using SFML and the SimpleAudioManager class. It creates a new window, loads a sound, runs a game loop at 60 frames per second, and plays the sound whenever the user presses the space key.

```
#include <SFML/Window.hpp>
#include "SimpleAudioManager.h"

int main() {
  sf::Window window(sf::VideoMode(320, 240), "AudioPlayback");
  sf::Clock clock;

  // Place your initialization logic here
  SimpleAudioManager audio;
  audio.Load("explosion.wav");

  // Start the game loop
  while (window.isOpen()) {
    // Only run approx 60 times per second
    float elapsed = clock.getElapsedTime().asSeconds();
    if (elapsed < 1.0f / 60.0f) continue;
    clock.restart();
    sf::Event event;
    while (window.pollEvent(event)) {
```

```
    // Handle window events
    if (event.type == sf::Event::Closed)
      window.close();

    // Handle user input
    if (event.type == sf::Event::KeyPressed &&
        event.key.code == sf::Keyboard::Space)
      audio.Play("explosion.wav");
  }
  // Place your update and draw logic here
  audio.Update(elapsed);
}
// Place your shutdown logic here
return 0;
}
```

Summary

In this chapter, we have seen some of the advantages of using the FMOD audio engine. We saw how to install the FMOD Ex Programmer's API in Visual Studio, how to initialize, manage, and release the FMOD sound system, how to load or stream an audio file of any type from disk, how to play a sound that has been previously loaded by FMOD, how to check for errors in every FMOD function, and how to create a simple audio manager that encapsulates the act of loading and playing audio files behind a simple interface.

3
Audio Control

In the previous chapter, we saw how to load and play audio files in FMOD. This time, we will explore some of the ways in which we can control the playback of those files. We will start with controlling the playback flow, by stopping the sound on demand, or seeking to different points in the audio file. Then we will cover how to modify the main properties of sound that were described in *Chapter 1*, *Audio Concepts*, such as volume and pitch. We will also see how FMOD lets us group sounds into categories, in order to control multiple sounds at once.

At the end of the chapter, we will expand the audio manager from the previous chapter, and make it more flexible and appropriate for use in games. This extended audio manager will provide a distinction between songs and sound effects, and handle each of them differently. We will see how to implement a fade in/fade out effect using simple volume manipulation, and how to add a variation to sound effects with a bit of randomness. The audio manager will also expose individual volume control for each category, making it easy to control from a game's option screen.

The channel handle

Let us start with a quick reminder from last chapter. When we use the `playSound()` method and pass the address of an `FMOD::Channel` pointer to the fourth parameter, we get a channel handle in return:

```
FMOD::Channel* channel;
system->playSound(FMOD_CHANNEL_FREE, sound, false, &channel);
```

Through this handle, we can control the sound in many ways. This handle remains valid while the sound has not finished playing, or until we explicitly stop the sound. If we try to perform an operation on the channel after the sound has stopped, nothing happens. Instead, the method we called returns an error stating that the channel handle is invalid, or already in use by another sound, if that is the case.

Something that might be confusing is that this FMOD channel is not the same type we talked back in *Chapter 1*, *Audio Concepts*, when we discussed multi-channel audio. This is simply the name FMOD gives to each of the slots it uses to play sounds simultaneously.

Controlling the playback

We already know how to play audio files, but it is also important to know how to stop them from playing. This is particularly important for looping sounds, because otherwise they would keep repeating forever. Usually, all we have to do is call the `stop()` method on the channel handle:

```
channel->stop();
```

When a sound stops playing—because it reached the end and it is not set to loop, or because we stopped it ourselves—its channel becomes free for other sounds to use. This means that once we stop a sound there is no way to resume it. If we need to stop a sound temporarily, and resume it at a later time, we need to use the `setPaused()` method:

```
// Pause the sound
channel->setPaused(true);
// Resume the sound
channel->setPaused(false);
```

Most methods that start with `set` are accompanied by an equivalent `get` method, such as `getPaused()`, that we can use to check the current value of that property. The following is a function that uses both methods in conjunction with each other, to toggle the paused state of a channel:

```
void TogglePaused(FMOD::Channel* channel) {
  bool paused;
  channel->getPaused(&paused);
  channel->setPaused(!paused);
}
```

Another common operation is to seek the sound to a different position in the file. This is done with the `setPosition()` method, which takes a number representing the position we want to seek to, and the units we are specifying that position in (milliseconds in the following example). This is useful if we want to make a sound start from the beginning after unpausing it:

```
channel->setPosition(0, FMOD_TIMEUNIT_MS);
```

Finally, if we have a looping sound, we can use the `setLoopCount()` method to control the number of times the sound should loop. The following example shows some of the possible parameters (with the default being `-1` to loop endlessly):

```
// Repeat endlessly
channel->setLoopCount(-1);
// Play once then, stop
channel->setLoopCount(0);
// Play three times, then stop
channel->setLoopCount(2);
```

Controlling the volume

Next, we will see how to control some of the main properties of sound, starting with its volume. This is done with a simple call to the `setVolume()` method, which takes a value ranging from `0` (silence) to `1` (maximum volume):

```
channel->setVolume(1.0f);
```

Similar to the way we paused the sound earlier, we can also silence it temporarily by using the `setMute()` method. Once we unmute the sound, it continues playing at its previous volume:

```
channel->setMute(true);
```

Both the methods preciously mentioned modify all channels of the sound simultaneously. On a sound with multiple channels, we can modify the volume of each channel separately, using the `setInputChannelMix()` method. This works for any amount of channels, by taking an array of volume levels as the first parameter, and the number of channels as the second. The following is an example for a stereo sound that mutes the left channel:

```
float levels[2] = {0.0f, 1.0f};
channel->setInputChannelMix(levels, 2);
```

Controlling the pitch

Controlling the pitch is not as straightforward as controlling the volume. We already know that modifying the frequency of a sound, changes its pitch and the channel handle actually has a `setFrequency()` method just for that:

```
channel->setFrequency(261.626f);
```

However, it does not work the way some of us might expect. For example, the middle C note on a piano has a frequency of approximately 261.626 Hz, so we might expect that setting the frequency to that value, would make the sound assume a pitch close to the middle C note, but this is not the case.

In order to understand this problem, let us first turn our attention to the getFrequency() method. If we call this method on a channel with its original frequency, what we get in return is actually the sampling rate of the sound. This means that any frequency values that we set must be relative to this value, or in other words, that any values above the original sampling rate of the sound will increase its pitch, and vice versa.

We could choose frequency values arbitrarily to get the desired effect, but an easier way to deal with pitch is in musical terms. In musical theory, the difference between two pitches is called an interval, with two of the most basic types of intervals being the octave, which corresponds to the distance between two consecutive notes with the same name, and the semitone, which corresponds to the distance between any two adjacent notes. The following are a few simple rules; we can modify an existing frequency by any of these intervals:

- Every time we multiply/divide a frequency by two we get a new frequency that sounds one octave higher/lower
- Every time we multiply/divide a frequency by two and a half we get new a frequency that sounds one semitone higher/lower

To make things easier, here are two helper methods that perform the previous calculations, given a frequency, and the number of octaves or semitones to change. Notice the use of the pow() function to apply the previous multiplications and divisions the necessary amount of times:

```
#include <math.h>

float ChangeOctave(float frequency, float variation) {
  static float octave_ratio = 2.0f;
  return frequency * pow(octave_ratio, variation);
}
float ChangeSemitone(float frequency, float variation) {
  static float semitone_ratio = pow(2.0f, 1.0f / 12.0f);
  return frequency * pow(semitone_ratio, variation);
}
```

Using these helper methods, it becomes simple to modify the pitch of a sound in FMOD in a meaningful way. For example, to decrease the pitch of a sound by 3 semitones, we could do the following:

```
float frequency;
channel->getFrequency(&frequency);
float newFrequency = ChangeSemitone(frequency, -3.0f);
channel->setFrequency(newFrequency);
```

Note that changing the frequency of the sound will also have the side effect of speeding it up or slowing it down. There is a way to change the pitch of a sound without affecting its speed in FMOD, but it requires using a DSP effect, which is outside the scope of this chapter. We will briefly cover DSP effects in the next chapter.

Controlling the panning

Finally, we can also control the panning of some sounds, as long as they are mono or stereo, and 2D (as the FMOD engine automatically positions 3D sounds). When these conditions are met, you can change the panning of the sound using the setPan() method, which takes any value from -1 (completely on the left) to 1 (completely on the right):

```
channel->setPan(-1.0f);
```

Panning works by modifying the volume of each output to give the illusion of position. However, the way FMOD calculates these values is different between mono and stereo sounds.

For mono sounds, the volume of each speaker follows a constant power curve that starts at 0 percent on one side, and goes to 100 percent on the other side, with the center position being at around 71 percent. This technique results in a smoother transition from one side to the other than using regular linear interpolation with 50 percent in the middle (because of the way we perceive sound intensity).

Stereo sounds, on the other hand, use a simpler formula referred to as setting the balance of the sound. Using this approach, both outputs are already at 100 percent in the center position, and panning to one side only decreases the volume of the opposite channel in a linear fashion. The following figure demonstrates both the approaches:

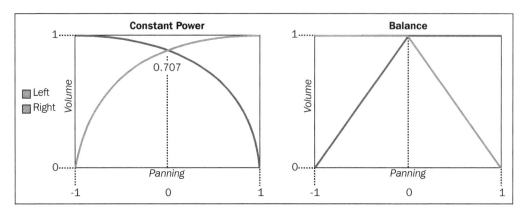

Grouping channels together

Another great feature of FMOD is that it lets us add different channels to a group and control them simultaneously. This is very useful for video games, where sound tends to fall into categories (such as background music, sound effects, or speech). To create a channel group we use the `createChannelGroup()` method of the system object:

```
FMOD::ChannelGroup* musicGroup;
system->createChannelGroup("music", &musicGroup);
```

Then we can easily add a channel to a group using the `setChannelGroup()` method of the channel object:

```
channel->setChannelGroup(musicGroup);
```

It is also possible to add a group as a child of another group, creating a hierarchy. This is done using the `addGroup()` method of the parent channel group object:

```
channelGroup->addGroup(anotherGroup);
```

There is also a global channel group called the master channel group, where every channel is placed every time you play a sound. You can get a reference to the master channel group by calling the `getMasterChannelGroup()` method of the system object:

```
FMOD::ChannelGroup* masterGroup;
system->getMasterChannelGroup(&masterGroup);
```

A good way to organize sounds in our games is to create a channel group for each category of sounds, and add all channel groups to the master channel group. This way we have control over individual categories, but we also have a way to control all sounds at once.

Controlling groups of channels

Most operations supported by channel groups are the same that we have seen already for individual channels. In particular, we can stop, pause, or mute all channels in a group, and control their volume and pitch. The syntax for these operations is the same as before, except for pitch, which is done through a setPitch() method, that instead of a frequency, takes any value between 0 and 10, and multiplies it by the current frequency.

```
// Calls stop on all channels in the group
channelGroup->stop();
// Mute or pause all channels
channelGroup->setMute(true);
channelGroup->setPaused(true);
// Halve the volume of all sounds in the group
channelGroup->setVolume(0.5f);
// Double the frequency of all sounds in the group
channelGroup->setPitch(2.0f);
```

All of these changes propagate down the channel group hierarchy automatically, without overwriting the values stored inside the channels. The way these values are applied depends on the type of operation.

For operations such as pausing and muting, the values in the channel group override the values in the children. This means that if the channel group is paused, every channel will remain paused regardless of their real values. On the other hand, if the channel group is not paused, the individual values in the channels are considered.

For volume and pitch, the values in the channel group are multiplied by the values in the children. For example, a channel at 80 percent volume inside a channel group at 50 percent volume will play at 40 percent volume instead.

Project 2 – improving the audio manager

In this project, we will build on top of the simple audio manager developed in the last chapter, and make it more flexible and game oriented. This time, besides loading and playing sounds, we will also be able to stop them and control their volume, which is necessary in almost every game. Furthermore, we will divide all sounds into two categories, each with its own set of features and behaviors:

- **Sound effects (SFXs)**: Sounds that are loaded into memory and do not loop. Multiple instances can be played at the same time. Their volume and pitch can be controlled directly, or randomized within a user-defined range, to add variation to the sound.

- **Songs**: Sounds that are streamed and set to loop. Only one song can be playing at any time. Transitions between songs are handled smoothly by the audio manager with volume fades.

Each game has its own needs, so you might want to create more categories, such as one for speech or ambient tracks.

Class definition

Once again, let us start with a listing of the class definition:

```cpp
#include <string>
#include <map>
#include <fmod.hpp>

class AudioManager {
 public:
  AudioManager();
  ~AudioManager();
  void Update(float elapsed);

  void LoadSFX(const std::string& path);
  void LoadSong(const std::string& path);

  void PlaySFX(const std::string& path,
               float minVolume, float maxVolume,
               float minPitch, float maxPitch);
  void PlaySong(const std::string& path);

  void StopSFXs();
  void StopSongs();
```

```
    void SetMasterVolume(float volume);
    void SetSFXsVolume(float volume);
    void SetSongsVolume(float volume);

 private:
  typedef std::map<std::string, FMOD::Sound*> SoundMap;
  enum Category { CATEGORY_SFX, CATEGORY_SONG, CATEGORY_COUNT };

  void Load(Category type, const std::string& path);

  FMOD::System* system;
  FMOD::ChannelGroup* master;
  FMOD::ChannelGroup* groups[CATEGORY_COUNT];
  SoundMap sounds[CATEGORY_COUNT];
  FMOD_MODE modes[CATEGORY_COUNT];

  FMOD::Channel* currentSong;
  std::string currentSongPath;
  std::string nextSongPath;

  enum FadeState { FADE_NONE,  FADE_IN, FADE_OUT };
  FadeState fade;
};
```

The class contains quite a few more members than the `SimpleAudioManager` class, but the basis is the same. To summarize the differences, we now have public methods to load, play, stop, and control the volume of sound effects and songs separately. Then, in the private portion of the class, we have an enumeration with the types of categories, and arrays of channel groups, sound maps, and modes, containing enough entries for each of the categories. Finally, there are some variables required to handle transitions between songs.

Initialization and destruction

In the constructor, besides initializing the sound system, we create one group channel for each sound category, and add them to the master channel group. We also initialize an array of modes describing how sounds in each category should be loaded. Finally, we seed the random number generator that will be used to play sound effects.

```
AudioManager::AudioManager() : currentSong(0), fade(FADE_NONE) {
  // Initialize system
  FMOD::System_Create(&system);
  system->init(100, FMOD_INIT_NORMAL, 0);
```

```
    // Create channels groups for each category
    system->getMasterChannelGroup(&master);
    for(int i = 0; i < CATEGORY_COUNT; ++i) {
      system->createChannelGroup(0, &groups[i]);
      master->addGroup(groups[i]);
    }

    // Set up modes for each category
    modes[CATEGORY_SFX] = FMOD_DEFAULT;
    modes[CATEGORY_SONG] = FMOD_DEFAULT | FMOD_CREATESTREAM |
                           FMOD_LOOP_NORMAL;

    // Seed random number generator for SFXs
    srand(time(0));
}
```

In the destructor, we do the same thing as we did in the simple audio manager, but this time there are multiple sound maps to clear.

```
AudioManager::~AudioManager() {
    // Release sounds in each category
    SoundMap::iterator iter;
    for(int i = 0; i < CATEGORY_COUNT; ++i) {
      for (iter = sounds[i].begin(); iter != sounds[i].end(); ++iter)
        iter->second->release();
      sounds[i].clear();
    }
    // Release system
    system->release();
}
```

Loading songs and sound effects

The loading portion of the manager is very similar to what we did in the last chapter. The public methods LoadSFX() and LoadSong() delegate their work to the private Load() method which does the actual loading process. The only difference is that the Load() method needs to use the correct sound map and mode from the arrays, based on the value of the first parameter:

```
void AudioManager::LoadSFX(const std::string& path) {
    Load(CATEGORY_SFX, path);
}
void AudioManager::LoadSong(const std::string& path) {
    Load(CATEGORY_SONG, path);
```

```
}
void AudioManager::Load(Category type, const std::string& path) {
  if (sounds[type].find(path) != sounds[type].end()) return;
  FMOD::Sound* sound;
  system->createSound(path.c_str(), modes[type], 0, &sound);
  sounds[type].insert(std::make_pair(path, sound));
}
```

Playing and stopping sound effects

Sound effects are the easier of the two categories to play. The `PlaySFX()` method takes the path of the sound, and a pair of minimum and maximum volume and pitch values. Then it searches for the sound in the correct map, and plays it back like before, except that it sets the volume and pitch of the sound using random values generated within the selected ranges:

```
void AudioManager::PlaySFX(const std::string& path,
                           float minVolume, float maxVolume,
                           float minPitch, float maxPitch) {
  // Try to find sound effect and return if not found
  SoundMap::iterator sound = sounds[CATEGORY_SFX].find(path);
  if (sound == sounds[CATEGORY_SFX].end()) return;

  // Calculate random volume and pitch in selected range
  float volume = RandomBetween(minVolume, maxVolume);
  float pitch = RandomBetween(minPitch, maxPitch);

  // Play the sound effect with these initial values
  FMOD::Channel* channel;
  system->playSound(FMOD_CHANNEL_FREE, sound->second,
                    true, &channel);
  channel->setChannelGroup(groups[CATEGORY_SFX]);
  channel->setVolume(volume);
  float frequency;
  channel->getFrequency(&frequency);
  channel->setFrequency(ChangeSemitone(frequency, pitch));
  channel->setPaused(false);
}
```

The preceding code makes use of two helper methods, `ChangeSemitone()` which was already shown earlier in this chapter, and `RandomBetween()` which can be seen in the following code snippet:

```
#include <stdlib.h>
#include <time.h>
```

```
float RandomBetween(float min, float max) {
  if(min == max) return min;
  float n = (float)rand()/(float)RAND_MAX;
  return min + n * (max - min);
}
```

Stopping all sound effects from playing is trivial to implement, thanks to the channel groups. You would typically call this when changing between scenes or opening a menu:

```
void AudioManager::StopSFXs() {
  groups[CATEGORY_SFX]->stop();
}
```

Playing and stopping songs

Songs are a bit harder to handle because we only want one to be playing at all times and we want transitions between them to happen smoothly. FMOD does not provide a way to fade the volume between sounds automatically, so we have to implement this manually with setVolume() calls within the Update() method. First, we need to create some member variables to store some states:

```
FMOD::Channel* currentSong;
std::string currentSongPath;
std::string nextSongPath;
enum FadeState { FADE_NONE,  FADE_IN,  FADE_OUT };
FadeState fade;
```

From the top, we need the channel handle to update the volume of the song, the path of the current song to ensure that we do not play the same song again, and the path of the next song to start playing it after the previous one finishes fading out. We also need a variable to store if we are currently fading in or fading out. The PlaySong() method follows these rules:

- If we are trying to play a song that is already playing, nothing should happen.
- If we are trying to play a song, but another song is already playing, we cannot start immediately. Instead, we instruct the manager to begin stopping the current song, and store the path of the song to play afterwards.

- If no song is playing, we can start the new song immediately, with its initial volume set to zero, and the manager set to the fade in state. The song must also be added to the correct channel group:

```
void AudioManager::PlaySong(const std::string& path) {
  // Ignore if this song is already playing
  if(currentSongPath == path) return;

  // If a song is playing stop them and set this as the next song
  if(currentSong != 0) {
    StopSongs();
    nextSongPath = path;
    return;
  }
  // Find the song in the corresponding sound map
  SoundMap::iterator sound = sounds[CATEGORY_SONG].find(path);
  if (sound == sounds[CATEGORY_SONG].end()) return;

  // Start playing song with volume set to 0 and fade in
  currentSongPath = path;
  system->playSound(FMOD_CHANNEL_FREE,
                    sound->second, true, &currentSong);
  currentSong->setChannelGroup(groups[CATEGORY_SONG]);
  currentSong->setVolume(0.0f);
  currentSong->setPaused(false);
  fade = FADE_IN;
}
```

- The `StopSongs()` method is significantly easier to implement, as it only needs to trigger a fade out if a song is playing, and clear any pending song request that was previously set:

```
void AudioManager::StopSongs() {
  if(currentSong != 0)
    fade = FADE_OUT;
  nextSongPath.clear();
}
```

It is in the `Update()` method where all of the fading takes place. The process follows these rules:

- If a song is playing and we are fading in, increase the volume of the current song a bit. Once the volume reaches one, stop fading.

- If a song is playing and we are fading out, decrease the volume of the current song a bit. Once the volume reaches zero, stop the song, and stop fading.

- If no song is playing, and there is a song set up to play next, start playing it:

```
void AudioManager::Update(float elapsed) {
  const float fadeTime = 1.0f; // in seconds
  if(currentSong != 0 && fade == FADE_IN) {
    float volume;
    currentSong->getVolume(&volume);
    float nextVolume = volume + elapsed / fadeTime;
    if(nextVolume >= 1.0f) {
      currentSong->setVolume(1.0f);
      fade = FADE_NONE;
    } else {
      currentSong->setVolume(nextVolume);
    }
  } else if(currentSong != 0 && fade == FADE_OUT) {
    float volume;
    currentSong->getVolume(&volume);
    float nextVolume = volume - elapsed / fadeTime;
    if(nextVolume <= 0.0f) {
      currentSong->stop();
      currentSong = 0;
      currentSongPath.clear();
      fade = FADE_NONE;
    } else {
      currentSong->setVolume(nextVolume);
    }
  } else if(currentSong == 0 && !nextSongPath.empty()) {
    PlaySong(nextSongPath);
    nextSongPath.clear();
  }
  system->update();
}
```

Controlling the master volume of each category

Controlling the master volume of each category is just a matter of calling the corresponding channel group method:

```
void AudioManager::SetMasterVolume(float volume) {
  master->setVolume(volume);
}
void AudioManager::SetSFXsVolume(float volume) {
  groups[CATEGORY_SFX]->setVolume(volume);
}
void AudioManager::SetSongsVolume(float volume) {
  groups[CATEGORY_SONG]->setVolume(volume);
}
```

Summary

In this chapter, we have seen how to control the playback of a sound, how to control the volume, pitch, and panning of a sound, how to control multiple sounds at once using channel groups, and finally how to apply these features in practical situations, such as fading between songs, or applying random variations to sound effects.

4
3D Audio

Our perception of sound varies depending on where we are located in relation to its source, and on several characteristics of the environment. We have already discussed that sound is a mechanical wave, which has an origin, and needs to travel all the way to our ears before we can hear it. Along the way, those sound waves interact with the environment, such as walls, objects, or the air itself, and begin to change. Many of the changes provide valuable cues for our brain to determine the location of the sound or the nature of the environment. The following is a list of some of the most important factors that have an impact on sound:

- **Distance**: The distance between the source of the sound and our ears has a significant effect on its intensity, because air and other mediums attenuate sound as it passes by.

- **Direction**: Our ears can identify the direction a sound is coming from thanks to minor time and intensity variations between the sounds captured by each ear.

- **Movement**: The relative speed between the sound source and our ears can make it appear to have a different pitch, because of a phenomenon known as the *Doppler effect*.

- **Room**: The size and shape of the room we are in can cause multiple echoes to accumulate, producing a reverberation effect, where sound seems to persist temporarily even after the original sound has stopped.

- **Obstacles**: Obstacles between the sound source and our ears tend to attenuate and muffle the sound. This is particularly true in the case of large obstacles such as walls.

In this chapter, we will explore the basics of 3D audio, which is the field of audio programming that tries to take some (or all) of these factors into consideration in order to produce a realistic audio simulation. This is one of the areas where using an audio engine such as FMOD really pays off, as it would be extremely difficult to implement some of these features ourselves.

Positional audio

The first aspect of 3D audio that we are going to work with (and perhaps the most important) is positional audio. **Positional audio** deals primarily with the location of each object that produces sound (which we will refer to as **audio sources**) in relation to or our ears (which we will refer to as the **audio listener**).

The first step required to create a 3D audio simulation is to describe every audio source and listener in the environment. Note that there is typically only one audio listener in a scene, unless we are creating a multiplayer split-screen type of game. The following figure shows an example of a scene with multiple audio sources and one audio listener in the middle:

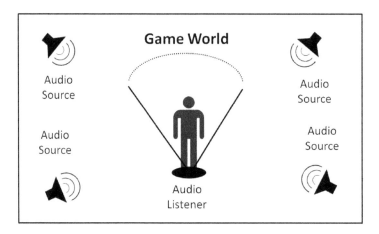

For each audio source and listener in the scene, we store information such as position, orientation, and velocity. Using this information, the audio engine produces a 3D audio simulation by modifying all the sounds in real time in several ways:

- **Position**: The volume of a source decreases and becomes muffled (by filtering the sound to attenuate some of the higher frequencies) as the distance to the listener increases. The formula used to calculate the volume of the sound given a distance is usually controllable by selecting a minimum and maximum distance, and a roll-off model.

- **Orientation**: Depending on the orientation of the listener in relation to each source, the audio engine simulates sound direction and position using speaker placement (for surround sound systems such as 5.1) or panning (for stereo sound systems). Audio sources can also be oriented, usually by defining a sound projection cone, with direction and angle information. Sound is then attenuated for listeners standing outside the range of the cone.

- **Velocity**: If the audio source is moving in relation to the listener, the pitch of the sound changes (increasing as the entities move closer and decreasing as the entities move apart) because of the Doppler effect. You can hear this effect in the real world, for example, when an ambulance passes next to you with its siren turned as soon as the ambulance moves past your location, there is a sudden drop in the pitch of the siren.

Positional audio in FMOD

Using positional audio in FMOD is not too different from what we have done so far. In fact, we have already used all the classes required for positional audio on the previous chapters; the FMOD::Channel class already works as an audio source, while the FMOD::System class controls all the audio listeners in the scene. Let us break down the entire process into steps.

Creating an audio source

The first point that we have to remember is to create our sounds using the FMOD_3D flag; otherwise, the 3D audio engine will not process them:

```
system->createSound("explosion.wav", FMOD_3D, 0, &sound);
```

Then we simply need to play the sounds as usual, storing a reference to the channel handle so that we can modify the 3D properties of the sound.

Setting the audio source's position and velocity

Once we play the sound and get back a channel handle, we can use it to set the position and velocity of the audio source with the set3DAttributes method:

```
FMOD_VECTOR position = { 3.0f, 4.0f, 2.0f };
FMOD_VECTOR velocity = { 1.0f, 0.0f, 0.0f };
channel->set3DAttributes(&position, &velocity);
```

We will typically set these values once when creating the audio source and update them every frame, or every time the game object associated with the audio source changes its position or velocity.

By default, the position is defined in meters, and the velocity is defined in meters per second (as we would typically see on a physics engine). We can change this scale by setting a different `distancefactor` parameter in the `System::set3DSettings` method.

Note that simply subtracting an object's position by its position on the previous frame does not yield a velocity in meters per second, as required. If we need to use this method, for example, because we do not know the actual velocity of the object, we have to multiply this delta by the time elapsed since the previous frame first (in seconds):

```
FMOD_VECTOR velocity;
velocity.x = (position.x - lastPosition.x) * elapsed;
velocity.y = (position.y - lastPosition.y) * elapsed;
velocity.z = (position.z - lastPosition.z) * elapsed;
```

Setting the audio source's direction

By default, every sound source is omnidirectional which means that the sound is emitted equally in every direction. We can give a sound source a direction, by defining a projection cone, using the `set3DConeOrientation` and `set3DConeSettings` methods:

```
FMOD_VECTOR direction = { 1.0f, 2.0f, 3.0f };
channel->set3DConeOrientation(&direction);
channel->set3DConeSettings(30.0f, 60.0f, 0.5f);
```

The `set3DConeOrientation` method takes a vector defining the main direction of the sound cone. The `set3DConeSettings` method takes three parameters, containing the inner angle, the outer angle, and the outer volume of the sound cone. The sound source is at full volume when the listener is within the inner angle, and attenuates towards the outer volume as the listener moves outside that angle.

Setting the audio source's range

We can control the overall distance where a sound is still audible with the `set3DMinMaxDistance` method:

```
channel->set3DMinMaxDistance(1.0f, 10000.0f);
```

We specify the range of the sound as a pair of values: the minimum distance and maximum distance. The minimum distance is the point at which the sound starts attenuating. If the listener is any closer to the source than the minimum distance, the sound will play at full volume. The maximum distance is the point at which the sound stops attenuating and its volume remains constant (a volume which is not necessarily zero).

The way volume varies between the minimum and maximum distance is known as the **rolloff model**. By default, FMOD uses a **logarithmic rolloff** that attenuates volume as a proportion of the minimum distance:

```
volume = min / distance;
```

By changing the minimum distance, we can control the overall size of the sound (for example, we could set a value of 0.1 for the sound of a fly, or a value of 500 for the sound of an explosion). When using this model, the maximum distance should have a large value, in order to give the sound enough distance to attenuate to silence. We can make the sound attenuate slower or faster by changing the `rolloffscale` parameter in the `System::set3DSettings` method.

The logarithmic model is realistic, but has the disadvantage of making it harder to calculate the full range of the sound, that is, the distance to silence. For this reason there are other models available that are easier to use, such as the `linear` rolloff model, which maps the minimum distance to full volume, the maximum distance to silence, and interpolates linearly in between. We can select the `linear` rolloff model when creating the sound by adding the `FMOD_3D_LINEARROLLOFF` flag. In this model, the system rolloff scale does nothing:

```
if (distance <= min) volume = 1.0
else if (distance >= max) volume = 0.0
else volume = (distance - min) / (max - min);
```

Setting the audio listener's properties

Finally, we must set the position, velocity, and orientation of the audio listener, using the `set3DListenerAttributes` method of the `system` object:

```
FMOD_VECTOR pos = { 3.0f, 4.0f, 2.0f };
FMOD_VECTOR vel = { 1.0f, 0.0f, 0.0f };
FMOD_VECTOR forward = { 1.0f, 0.0f, 0.0f };
FMOD_VECTOR up = { 0.0f, 1.0f, 0.0f };
system->set3DListenerAttributes(0, &pos, &vel, &forward, &up);
```

This is very similar to setting up the attributes for an audio source, except for the added orientation. The orientation is specified as a pair of normalized, perpendicular vectors, pointing in the up and forward directions of the listener (which you will typically get from your camera object or from the view transformation matrix).

The first parameter is an index that identifies the audio listener. By default, there is only one audio listener in the scene, so we use the value of 0. If we need more than one audio listener, we can use the `set3DNumListeners` method of the `system` object to increase that number.

Integration with a game

There are several ways to approach this problem, depending on the architecture used by the game engine, but in general, the process is to assign an audio source to each game object that can emit a sound, and assign an audio listener to the camera object. Then, in the update phase of our game loop, every time we change the position, velocity, or orientation of a game object or camera, we must follow it up with an update to the corresponding audio structures. Finally, at the end of the update phase, we update the audio system, which processes all the changes made to the sources and listeners and updates the simulation accordingly.

Reverb

Positional audio (with its attenuation, speaker placement, and Doppler effect) comprises the most fundamental level of 3D audio. Now we will cover some advanced techniques that we can use on top of positional audio to provide a more complete simulation of how sounds interact with the environment. One of those techniques is called **reverberation**, or **reverb**.

Reverb is the capability of sound to persist in a particular space for some time after the original sound has stopped. We can think of reverb as a succession of echoes with very little time in between them.

Reverb occurs because most audio sources project sound in several directions at once. Some of those sound waves reach our ears directly, in the shortest path possible. Others, however, head in different directions, and reflect off various surfaces, such as walls, before finally reaching our ears. These reflected sound waves take longer to reach our ears than the direct sound waves, and become quieter with every bounce they make. The combination of all the reflected sound waves creates the effect of reverb.

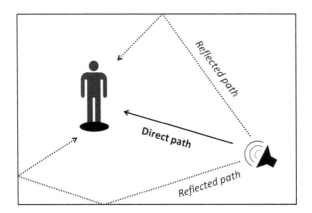

Simulating reverb in a game can enhance the realism of a scene because it provides strong cues about the size and nature of the environment. For example, an empty cathedral with large, reflective walls will usually result in a lot of reverb. On the other hand, an outdoor location with no walls will have virtually no reverb. We can also infer the size of a room from the duration of the reverb, since sound waves have to travel longer in a large room than in a small room.

Reverb in FMOD

If we are already using positional audio in our scene, adding reverb in FMOD requires only a few extra lines of code.

Creating a reverb object

First, we need to create an `FMOD::Reverb` object using the `createReverb` method:

```
FMOD::Reverb* reverb;
system->createReverb(&reverb);
```

This creates a reverb zone that automatically applies reverb to every sound that a listener can hear when standing inside that zone. You can safely create more than one reverb zone simultaneously, as FMOD automatically combines their effects.

To disable a reverb zone, you can use the `setActive` method. Alternatively, if you do not need that zone any more, you can destroy it permanently with the `release` method:

```
reverb->setActive(false);      // Disable temporarily
reverb->release();             // Destroy reverb
```

Setting reverb properties

A reverb has many properties to customize its behavior. These properties are defined inside the `FMOD_REVERB_PROPERTIES` structure, and can be applied to the reverb object using the `setProperties` method. Fortunately, FMOD also provides a set of presets that you can use directly, such as `FMOD_PRESET_CONCERTHALL`:

```
FMOD_REVERB_PROPERTIES properties = FMOD_PRESET_CONCERTHALL;
reverb->setProperties(&properties);
```

Setting reverb position and radius

We can specify the position and range of the reverb using the `set3DAttributes` method. The range of the reverb is specified with a minimum radius (reverb is at full volume within that radius) and a maximum radius (reverb is disabled outside that radius).

```
FMOD_VECTOR position = { 10.0f, 0.0f, 0.0f };
reverb->set3DAttributes(&position, 10.0f, 20.0f);
```

Setting the default ambient reverb

We can also set which reverb properties to use when the listener is not inside any reverb zone, using the `setReverbAmbientProperties` method of the `system` object.

```
FMOD_REVERB_PROPERTIES properties = FMOD_PRESET_OFF;
system->setReverbAmbientProperties(&properties);
```

Obstruction and occlusion

Obstacles in the environment, such as large objects, or walls, also alter the way we perceive sound. We can often hear a person speaking in an adjacent room, but the sound is not as clear as if they were standing next to us. The reason for this is that although sound can pass through several types of materials, it loses energy and several of its higher frequencies during the process. This results in a quieter, muffled sound. There are two techniques used to simulate obstacles in 3D audio: **obstruction** and **occlusion**.

Obstruction occurs when the source and the listener are in the same environment, and there is an obstacle in the way, but there is still enough space around the obstacle for the sound waves to flow. In this situation, sound waves passing directly through the obstacle are attenuated and filtered, but reflected sound waves are not affected.

Occlusion occurs when the source and listener are in different environments, and all the sound needs to go through an obstacle, such as a wall, before reaching the listener. In this situation, both direct and reflected sound waves are attenuated and filtered.

The filter applied to the obstructed or occluded sound waves is usually a low pass filter, which attenuates the higher frequencies, resulting in a muffled sound.

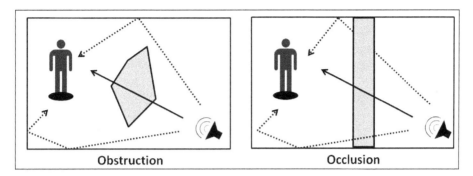

Obstruction   Occlusion

Obstruction and occlusion in FMOD

We can simulate obstruction and occlusion in FMOD using the built-in geometry engine. This only works if we already have our audio sources and listeners set up. Afterwards, we need to create geometry objects to represent the obstacles in our environment.

The easiest way to create these objects is to start from a 3D triangle mesh representation of our obstacle. Then we create an instance of `FMOD::Geometry` with enough space to store all of our triangles and vertices, using the `createGeometry` method:

```
FMOD::Geometry* geometry;
system->createGeometry(numTriangles, numVertices, &geometry);
```

Next, for each triangle in our mesh, we add a new polygon to the geometry object using the `addPolygon` method. The first two parameters control the amount of obstruction and occlusion to perform. The third parameter decides if the polygon should be double sided. The fourth parameter is the number of vertices in the polygon, and the fifth parameter is the polygon data itself. The sixth parameter returns an index which can be used to perform further operations on the polygon.

```
FMOD_VECTOR vertices[3]; // Fill with triangle vertices
int polygonIndex; // Gets an index for the new polygon
geometry->addPolygon(0.5f, 0.5f, false, 3, vertices,
&polygonIndex);
```

We should create the polygon using vertices in object space, not in world space. Then, in order to position the geometry the world, we can use a combination of the `setPosition`, `setRotation`, and `setScale` methods.

Effects

Besides all of the 3D audio simulations described earlier, there is another subject that we should cover: DSP effects. A **DSP** effect (which stands for **digital signal processing**) is an algorithm that takes sound data as input, modifies it in some way, and returns a new set of data as output. Most effects either manipulate the amplitudes or frequencies of the sound data, or add multiple sounds together (frequently that sound is a delayed and attenuated version of itself). The following is a list of some common types of DSP effects:

- **Normalize**: This effect scales the volume of the sound so that the peak amplitude is at the maximum volume level.

- **Compressor**: This effect makes the loud sections of the sound quieter, then brings the entire volume up to compensate, reducing the dynamic range of the sound

- **Distortion**: This effect distorts the sound, making it sound harsher

- **Low-pass filter**: This effect attenuates all frequencies in the sound above a certain range, making the sound muffled

- **High-pass filter**: This effect attenuates all frequencies in the sound below a certain range, making the sound thinner

- **Parametric EQ**: This effect provides complex volume control over all different ranges of frequencies in the sound

- **Delay**: In this effect the sound plays once, and keeps repeating after a certain amount of time, until it runs out of energy

- **Echo**: In this effect a delay with a duration that is long enough for us to perceive as separate sounds

- **Flanger**: This effect doubles the sound with a very small delay between each instance, and varies this delay over time

- **Chorus**: This effect plays multiple instances of the sound together, with small pitch and time variations between them

- **Pitch shift**: This effect changes the pitch of a sound without altering its playback speed

- **Noise removal**: This effect silences every value below a certain volume threshold

Effects in FMOD

Once again, we will only cover the very basics here. The easiest way to create a DSP effect in FMOD is to use the `createDSPByType` method, with one of the available DSP types as a parameter (check the FMOD documentation for the complete list of types).

```
FMOD::DSP* dsp;
system->createDSPByType(FMOD_DSP_TYPE_ECHO, &dsp);
```

This returns an `FMOD::DSP` object that you can apply to any channel, channel group, or the `system` object itself, using the `addDSP` method of the corresponding object. You can also add more than one DSP effect to the same object, which chains them together automatically:

```
channel->addDSP(dsp, 0);
```

The second parameter allows more control over the DSP connection, but we will ignore it for our simple examples.

Finally, most DSP effects have a set of parameters that you can control using the `setParameter` method (once again, check the documentation for a list of all the available parameters):

```
dsp->setParameter(FMOD_DSP_ECHO_DECAYRATIO, 0.75f);
```

Example 1 – time stretching

As our first application of DSP effects, here is an example that shows how to change the playback speed of a sound without affecting its pitch. To do this, we need to combine a regular frequency change, which modifies both the pitch and the speed of the sound, with a pitch shift DSP effect, in order to return the pitch back to normal.

```
// Play at half speed
float amount = 0.5f;

// Modify frequency which changes both speed and pitch
float frequency;
channel->getFrequency(&frequency);
channel->setFrequency(frequency * amount);

// Create a pitch shift DSP to get pitch back to normal
// by applying the inverse amount
FMOD::DSP* dsp;
system->createDSPByType(FMOD_DSP_TYPE_PITCHSHIFT, &dsp);
dsp->setParameter(FMOD_DSP_PITCHSHIFT_PITCH, 1.0f / amount);
```

```
dsp->setParameter(FMOD_DSP_PITCHSHIFT_FFTSIZE, 4096);

// Now only the speed will change
channel->addDSP(dsp, 0);
```

Example 2 – simple radio effect

You can also combine multiple effects to achieve behaviors that are more complicated. For example, here is a rudimentary radio effect simulation, which works by applying a distortion and a high pass filter to the sound.

```
FMOD::DSP* distortion;
system->createDSPByType(FMOD_DSP_TYPE_DISTORTION, &distortion);
distortion->setParameter(FMOD_DSP_DISTORTION_LEVEL, 0.85f);

FMOD::DSP* highpass;
system->createDSPByType(FMOD_DSP_TYPE_HIGHPASS, &highpass);
highpass->setParameter(FMOD_DSP_HIGHPASS_CUTOFF, 2000.0f);

channel->addDSP(distortion, 0);
channel->addDSP(highpass, 0);
```

The distortion simulates the loss of information that often occurs when transmitting analog signals and the high pass filter makes the sound thinner by getting rid of the lower frequencies.

Summary

In this chapter, we have seen how to simulate sound coming from specific locations in the environment, how to simulate reverb from reflected sound waves, how to simulate obstruction and occlusion from obstacles, and finally how to apply DSP effects to sounds.

5
Intelligent Audio

Up to this point, we have played sounds in a very linear fashion; we load an audio file from a disk and play it when needed, optionally controlling some of its parameters during playback. Even when we used advanced features such as 3D audio, there was still a one-to-one relationship between the sound and the audio file.

However, a sound does not necessarily correspond to a single audio file. In many scenarios we can benefit from using multiple audio files for a single sound. For example, we can often reduce repetition by providing several variations of the same sound as separate audio files, or we can build complex soundscapes by combining several smaller sound fragments.

For other sounds, the modifications we apply at runtime to their parameters are just as important as the audio files that compose them. For example, we cannot realistically simulate the sound of a car engine without constantly updating its pitch and volume based on the engine's rpm and load values. Another common example is to have a soundtrack dynamically react to the events in the game in order to convey more or less tension to the player.

As programmers, we could certainly implement any of these features by writing specialized code for each situation, orchestrating each audio file and sound parameter as necessary. However, this approach takes a significant amount of effort, and is hard to manage and tweak, since most of the behavior gets hardcoded into the game. An even bigger problem is that it is usually a sound designer, not a programmer, which creates the sounds for a game, and using this approach would require a significant amount of communication and synchronization between both parties.

Thankfully, we can solve this problem by using a high-level audio engine. These engines usually provide an external tool that the sound designer can use to create complex sounds, independently from a programmer, and store them as sound events. Then, regardless of the complexity of the sound, the programmer can easily trigger it from the game, usually by writing the name of the event.

The main difficulty in covering this topic is that there are several high-level audio engines available, and each of them has its own set of features and philosophy. Using these tools, we can perform things such as generative audio (generating audio at runtime from a set of sound samples and rules) or adaptive music (music that changes depending on game events). To simplify the terminology, we will be using the term intelligent audio to encompass all situations where a sound can have complex behavior attached to it.

In this chapter, we will work with the FMOD Designer tool and see some of the interesting stuff that we can do with it. A detailed coverage of the tool would be impossible given the limited scope of the book, but it should be enough to give you some ideas and to get you started. For more information, the FMOD Designer tool ships with a user manual that is over 400 pages long, and a sample project with many examples.

Audio files versus sound events

Before installing the FMOD Designer tool, let us start by really understanding the difference between treating each audio file as a sound, and working at a higher level of abstraction with sound events (or sound cues in some engines). The following figure demonstrates how we have been approaching audio in our games so far:

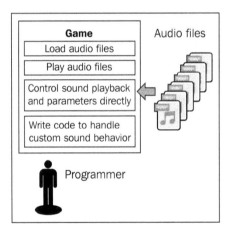

In this model, we can see that the game interacts directly with the audio files, and that the code is responsible for using these audio files in a way that is appropriate for the game, which usually requires the creation of specialized codes. When we move over to using a high-level audio engine such as the FMOD Designer, the process is significantly different, as we can see in the following figure:

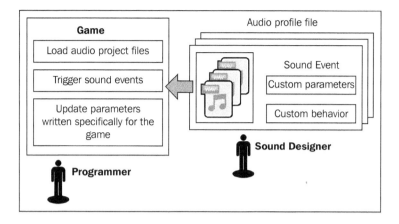

The first difference in this model is that the game does not interact directly with audio files. Instead, it interacts with entities known as sound events, which may contain multiple audio files, and encapsulate all of the custom behavior and parameters of the sound that were previously inside the game. This separation makes the game code a lot simpler, and provides a better environment for a sound designer to work.

Notice also, that there is an audio project file that groups all sound events together. This means that the game only needs to load this single file to get access to all sound events, which is significantly easier than having to load every individual audio file.

Introducing the FMOD Designer

The FMOD Designer is the high-level, data-driven API that complements the FMOD Ex low-level engine that we have been using so far. It contains two parts:

- **FMOD Designer**: This is a sound designer tool that allows us to create complex sound events and interactive music for our games (from `http://www.fmod.org`)

- **FMOD Event System**: This is an application layer that lets us use the content created with the designer within our games (comes bundled with FMOD Ex, inside the `fmoddesignerapi` folder)

The FMOD Designer projects have the `.fdp` extension, but to use them inside of a game you must first build them from the **Project** menu. The build process generates a `.fev` file, containing all the information for every sound event in the project, and one `.fsb` file for each wave bank in the project, which is where the audio files are stored. The following is a screenshot of the FMOD Designer user interface:

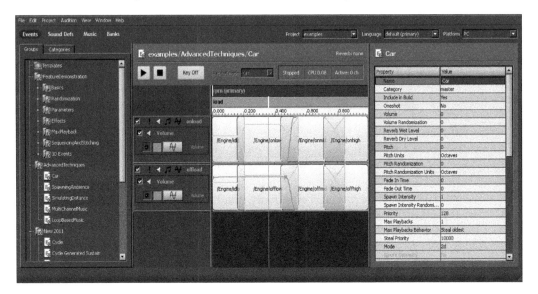

The most important task of the FMOD Designer is to create sound events. There are two types of sound events in FMOD, and an interactive music system:

- **Simple events**: With simple events, we can create sounds composed by multiple audio files, and play them randomly or sequentially, one or several at a time, at different rates, and with random volume or pitch variation

- **Multi-track events**: With multi-track events, we can combine as many simple events as we need (in this case called **sound defs**), organize them into layers, apply effects to them, control which sound defs should be playing at any given time, create custom parameters, and link those parameters to any of the properties of the sound or effects

- **Interactive music**: With the interactive music system, we can create songs (called **cues**) composed by multiple segments, and have the game transition between them in response to certain events. Besides transitions, we can also add flourishes to the music, which play concurrently and synchronized with the main song

Over the next few sections, we will briefly cover the main features and user interface of the first two of these systems, as well as some ideas and examples of how to use them in the context of a game. Coverage of the topic of interactive music will have to be more superficial, because its breadth exceeds the scope of this book.

Simple events

Simple events are the easiest to use, as well as the least resource intensive. We should therefore try to use simple events whenever they are enough for our requirements. With a simple event, we can:

- Create a sound composed by multiple audio files
- Play audio files sequentially or in a random order
- Randomize sound properties, such as volume or pitch
- Control the looping behavior of the sound
- Play multiple audio files at once, or at certain intervals

To create a simple event, go to the **Events** section, right-click on top of any **Event Group**, and then select the **Add Simple Event** option. If there is no **Event Group** created, we can create one from the same context menu. Event groups behave like folders and serve to organize all of our events:

With the event selected, the next step is to add the audio files that compose it to the **Playlist** pane, either through the right-click context menu, or by dragging some audio files into it. If we intend to play the audio files in a random order, we can specify the probability of each file playing through the right-click context menu, or using the dial control at the bottom-left corner of the pane:

On the **Playlist Options** pane, we can control how the audio engine should pick files from the playlist. There are three different **Playlist Behaviors**:

- **Random**: This option picks an audio file at random every time, following the weights attributed in the playlist to each of them. We can also select whether to allow the same audio file to play twice in a row.

- **Shuffle**: This option randomizes the playlist once, and then plays the audio files in that order.

- **Sequential**: This option follows the same order in which the audio files appear in the playlist.

Inside the **Playlist Options** pane, we can also find a **Sound Randomization** section, which lets us apply some variation to the starting volume and pitch of each file (similar to what we implemented ourselves back in *Chapter 3, Audio Control*):

In the **Playback Options** pane, which controls how many audio files, should be played and how often, there are four different **Playback Modes**:

- **Oneshot**: This mode picks a single audio file, and plays it only once
- **Repeating Loop**: This mode picks a single audio file, and plays it multiple times (with the number of times being controlled by the **Play Count** parameter)
- **Successive Loop**: This mode plays multiple audio files in succession, picking a new one each time (with the number of files to play being controlled by the **Loop Count** parameter)
- **Granular**: This mode is similar to the previous mode, but allows us to control the time to wait between each file that is played (**Grain Interval** parameter), how many files can be playing simultaneously (**Polyphony** parameter), and the total amount of files to play before the sound ends (**Total Grains** parameter)

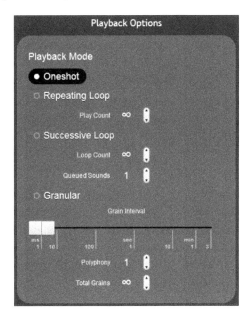

Finally, there is the **Properties** pane on the right side of the interface, which allows us to control several other properties of the sound event, such as most of the 3D audio properties discussed on the previous chapter.

Examples of simple events

Here are some ideas of how we can use simple events to enrich the audio in our games. Most of these ideas can be found on the examples project that comes with the FMOD Designer, so be sure to look there too.

Avoiding repetitive sound effects

Most games have a few sound effects that are played all the time, such as the sound of a character's footsteps, or the sound of a gun. If we use the exact same audio file every time, the player will usually notice the repetition after some time, which is undesirable in most cases. Using simple events, we can easily make these sound effects more interesting and dynamic, just by providing a few variations of the sound and letting the audio engine pick one randomly.

Adding a very small volume and pitch variation to the sound can also do wonders, as long as the variation is not large enough to change the overall nature of the sound. Values along the lines of -3 dB for the volume and +/- 2 semitones for the pitch are usually good starting points.

Creating a footsteps sound loop

There are several ways we can use a footsteps sound effect in a game. For example, we could have an audio file containing the sound of a single footstep, and trigger it once for every step the character takes inside the game world, or we could have a looping audio file with a walking sound, and play it constantly whenever the character is walking.

The first approach requires more work inside the game, while the second approach takes more memory, as the audio file needs to be longer. Using a simple event, we can combine both approaches, by taking an audio file of a single footstep, and setting up the event so that it performs the looping, using time intervals that are appropriate for a certain walking speed. Later, when working with multi-track events, we will also see a way to vary the walking speed dynamically.

We start by creating a simple event with the footstep audio files (following the advices given earlier in order to avoid repetition) and set the playback mode to granular. Then we adjust the grain interval so that the time between each footstep corresponds to the speed of the character walking, and increase the polyphony so that each footstep can sound without having to wait for the previous to end. We can also set slightly different maximum and minimum grain interval values, to reinforce the variations of the sound even further.

Creating a breaking glass sound effect

Another approach we can use to reduce repetition in our sound effects is to generate them at runtime as a combination of a few smaller sound fragments. For example, to simulate the sound of a glass object falling to the ground and shattering, we could have a pool of different glass breaking sounds, and always play two or three of them in quick succession. Combined with the usual volume and pitch variations, the result is a sound effect that will sound different most of the time.

To implement this type of sound effect, we need to use the granular playback mode, and set both the polyphony and the grain count parameters to the number of sound fragments that we want to use at once. For the breaking glass sound effect, we could set the polyphony and grain count to 2 or 3, and set a very small grain interval (for example, 200 ms), so that the sounds play almost at the same time.

Creating an ambient track of singing birds

The same technique used to generate the sound of a glass breaking can also generate long, looping, and ever changing, ambient tracks. A common example is to take a few small audio files of birds singing, and by triggering them randomly at different times, and with different volume and pitch, we can easily give the impression of being in a forest, where there are several different birds singing. The process is very similar to the previous effect, except that this time we should set a large polyphony (such as 15), a grain interval value of around 1s, and an infinite grain count so that the sound does not stop playing. Modifying the 3D position randomization properties can also be useful to create a volumetric sound, and give the impression that every bird is located in a different point in space, instead of every sound coming from the same spot.

Multi-track events

Multi-track events are significantly more powerful than simple events. In fact, before adding any sound to a multi-track event, we must turn it into a sound def, which has almost the same functionality as a simple event. With a multi-track event, we can:

- Perform everything that we could with a simple event
- Create multiple layers of sounds that play at the same time
- Apply one or more DSP effects to each layer
- Create custom parameters to modify the sound in real-time
- Play different sounds depending on the value of a parameter
- Modify any of the sound or effect properties from a parameter

Before creating a multi-track event, we must prepare a sound def for each of the sounds that we intend to use. The process is similar to creating a simple event, although the interface is a bit different. Head over to the **Sound Defs** section, right-click on top of any folder, and select one of the **Add sound def** options:

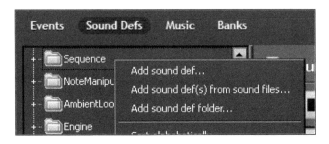

The interface used to create a sound def is a bit like a condensed version of the simple event interface, with the playlist on the left, and every other property on the right. Since most of the properties control something that we have already seen in simple events, there is no need to repeat that information here:

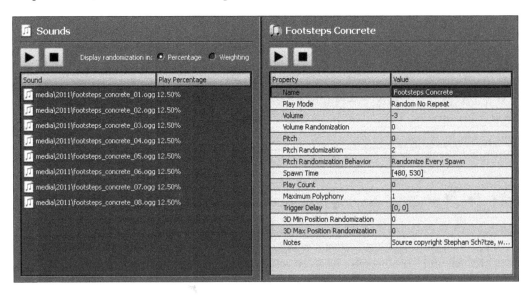

To create a multi-track event, follow the same steps used to create a simple event, but select the **Add Multi-Track Event** option instead:

A multi-track event is divided into layers, or tracks, with each layer being able to contain multiple sound defs. Adding a new layer, or adding sound to a layer, are both handled by right-clicking on the following interface and selecting the **Add layer** or **Add sound** option from the context menu:

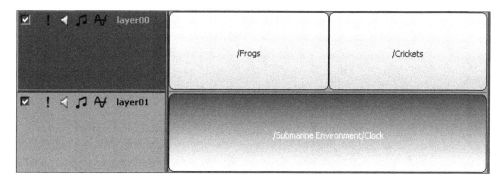

By default, the preceding example will play all three sound defs at the same time. This behavior changes as soon as we add a parameter to the sound, which can be done by right-clicking on the dark area on top of the sounds region, and selecting the **Add parameter** option from the list:

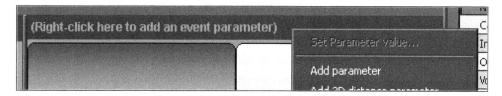

A parameter is essentially a variable with a certain range of permitted values that the game code can modify. The way the FMOD Designer represents parameters might look like a timeline, but it is important to understand that a parameter is a generic value, and does not necessarily represent time.

The first parameter we create is marked as the **primary** parameter, and it determines which sounds to play. In the following example, only the two sounds that are in contact with the red line (representing the current value of the **primary** parameter) will be playing. Changing the value of the parameter to any value above 0.5 would replace the **Frogs** sound with the **Crickets** sound. We can create multiple parameters in the same event, although only one of them will be marked as primary:

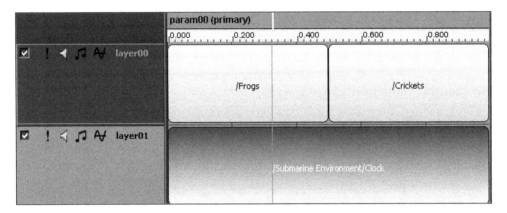

Another use of parameters is to control the sound properties of each layer. In order to do that, we must first add an effect to the layer we want to control, by right-clicking on the layer, and selecting the **Add effect** option. Effects can vary from a simple volume or pitch control, to more complex DSP effects, such as a distortion or a delay:

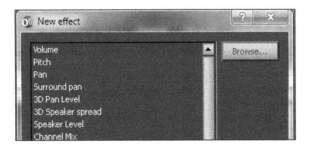

Having an effect added to a layer, and a parameter selected, we can draw curves on the layer, which represent how the properties of the effect should vary with the values of the parameter. In the following example, we have added a second parameter to the event, which modifies the pitch of the first layer, and the volume of the second layer:

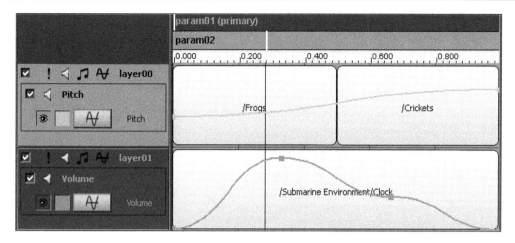

Finally, by right-clicking on any sound inside a multi-track event, we can access some sound instance properties that are not available elsewhere. Among those properties, there is an auto pitch feature, which behaves like adding a pitch effect to that sound, and controlling it based on a parameter, but is simpler to use. This feature is useful when trying to simulate the sound of a car engine:

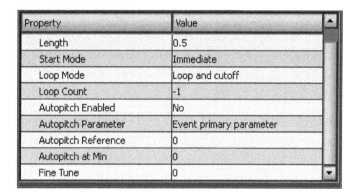

Property	Value
Length	0.5
Start Mode	Immediate
Loop Mode	Loop and cutoff
Loop Count	-1
Autopitch Enabled	No
Autopitch Parameter	Event primary parameter
Autopitch Reference	0
Autopitch at Min	0
Fine Tune	0

Examples of multi-track events

Here are some ideas of how we can use multi-track events to provide a more interactive and dynamic game audio experience in our games. Many of these ideas build upon the ones discussed earlier for simple events.

Creating an interactive footsteps sound loop

One of the simple event examples from the previous section described how to generate a looping footsteps sound. However, that sound was only useful for a specific walking speed, and for a specific surface. Using multi-track events, we can create a single sound event that contains footstep sounds for all different types of surfaces, such as grass, concrete, or sand, and allow the game to control the walking speed through a parameter.

In order to do this, we must first create a sound def for each type of surface the character can walk on. Each sound def should play a footsteps sound loop at the average walking speed, which we can control with the spawn rate parameter (this speed should be consistent between each sound def).

Then, we must create a multi-track event with a single layer, and two parameters to control the surface type (primary) and the walking speed. By adding all the sounds to this layer, distributing them evenly (by right-clicking and selecting the **Layout sounds evenly** option), and setting the maximum range of the surface type parameter to be the total number of sounds in the layer, we can use that parameter as a simple index to select which surface the character is walking on.

For the walking speed parameter, we need to add an effect of type Spawn Intensity to the layer, and draw a curve to control how the spawn intensity relates to the walking speed parameter. For example, a value of 0.5 means that the footsteps will occur at half the average speed, while a value of 2.0 means that footsteps will occur at twice the average speed.

Simulating the sound of a car engine

We can also use multi-track events to generate complex interactive sounds, such as the sound of a car engine. The FMOD Designer examples project has a great car engine simulation that we can study. That sound event has two layers, and two parameters, one for the engine's rpm, and one for the engine's load.

Each of the layers contains four different sounds, recorded from a car engine at different rpm ranges. The sounds on the top layer correspond to the car accelerating (on-load), while the sounds on the bottom layer correspond to the car decelerating (off-load).

The load parameter serves to blend between both layers at runtime with a volume effect. When the load parameter is in the middle, we hear a mix of both layers, but as the load parameter changes, the volumes quickly change so that we only hear one of the layers.

The `rpm` parameter serves two purposes. As the primary parameter, it determines which of the four sounds should be playing for the current value. The sounds actually overlap at the edges, so at certain rpm values, we can hear a mix of two sounds at once. The other purpose of the `rpm` parameter is to modify the pitch of the sound, so that higher the rpm value, the higher is the pitch of the sound. This is handled automatically by enabling the **auto-pitch** feature on each of the sounds:

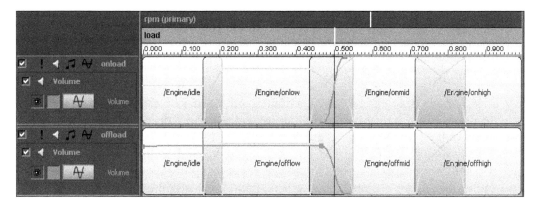

Creating a complex ambient track of a forest

Using a simple event, we were able to create a looping ambient track with a large number of singing birds. Using a multi-track event, we can easily extend the ambient track to contain other layer of sounds. For example, we could add a layer with the sound of the wind looping in the background, and layers for other types of animal cries, probably occurring at different rates than the bird sounds.

If we wanted to simulate a cave within the forest, we could create a parameter to control the location of the character, and add an occlusion effect to every layer that is only active for a certain range of values.

Additionally, we could create a parameter to specify the time of the day, and play different sounds depending on its value, such as removing the sounds of the birds at night, and bringing some cricket sounds in.

Interactive music

In the same way that we can create complex sound effects that change depending on the events of the game, it is also possible to do the same for the game's background music. This allows the music to adapt to the circumstances, for example, to convey the correct emotion for the moment, or provide a sense of tension when danger draws near.

Music that is played in a non-linear fashion like this is known as interactive music (if the player directly controls the changes) or adaptive music (if the music reacts to the game environment, but not necessarily to the player). There are two main approaches to creating interactive music.

The vertical approach (re-orchestration)

In this approach, the audio system modifies the mix of the song in real-time depending on events occurring in the game. This can consist, for example, of adding new instruments to the song, or making the music play faster or slower to match the gameplay.

The easiest way to implement this type of interactive music in the FMOD Designer is by using multi-track events in combination with specially prepared multi-channel audio files (which we can create using audio editing software, such as Audacity). This usually requires splitting up the music into layers, and adding each of the layers to a different audio channel in the file. Then, using the Channel Mix effect on a multi-track event, we can easily control the individual volumes of each audio channel based on the value of a parameter.

The most common application of this technique is to create a `tension` or `excitement` parameter, so that the song gets more intense (by adding more layers) as the value increases. The famous Japanese composer, Koji Kondo, is very fond of creating interactive music using this approach. Some recent examples include:

- On the Super Mario Galaxy levels where Mario rides on top of a star ball, the speed at which Mario moves completely determines the pitch, playback rate, and even the amount of instruments playing in the song.

- On the market area of The Legend of Zelda: Skyward Sword, each merchant has its own variation of the market theme. As the link approaches one of the merchants, the music changes very smoothly into the corresponding variation (while retaining the correct relative positioning within the theme).

The horizontal approach (re-sequencing)

In this approach, the music moves or jumps between different sections depending on the events of the game. This usually requires splitting the music into segments, so that the game can transition between them. When the system is not transitioning between segments, it keeps looping the current segment, and the music continues playing indefinitely.

Information about the tempo and time signature of the music is frequently required, so that the audio system can synchronize transitions to beats or measures of the song to provide a more musical experience. The interactive music system in the FMOD Designer is capable of creating interactive music sequences in this fashion.

A classic example of interactive music using the horizontal approach is the song, *A pirate I was meant to be*, in *Monkey Island 3*, where the player can actually select, in real-time, what verse of the song the characters will sing next. The song waits in a loop while the player makes his choice, and transitions gracefully afterwards.

Calling sound events from the game code

In order to test our FMOD Designer project in a game, we must first build the project, by selecting the **Build from the Project** menu, or pressing *Ctrl + B*. This process will generate the `fev` and `fsb` files that we have to copy to our game assets folder.

Next, we have to add some extra dependencies to our C++ project, so that we can interact with the FMOD Designer API. These dependencies ship together with the FMOD Ex Programmer's API, but we must add the references ourselves, as follows:

1. Navigate to **C/C++ | General**, and add `C:\FMOD\ fmoddesignerapi\api\ inc` to the list of **Additional Include Directories** (entries are separated by semicolons).

2. Navigate to **Linker | General**, and add `C:\FMOD\ fmoddesignerapi\api\ lib` to the list of **Additional Library Directories**.

3. Navigate to **Linker | Input**, and add `fmod_event.lib` to the list of **Additional Dependencies**.

4. Navigate to **Build Events | Post-Build Event**, and add `xcopy /y "C:\FMOD\ fmoddesignerapi\api\fmod_event.dll" "$(OutDir)"` to the **Command Line** list.

5. Include the `<fmod_event.hpp>` header file from your code.

Finally, the process of loading an FMOD Designer project, playing a sound event, and modifying some of its parameters, is in many ways similar to what we saw in *Chapter 2, Audio Playback*. Let us take a look at the most basic way to do it.

First, we must create and initialize an FMOD::EventSystem object, and load the project file. We should also call the update() method in every frame, and the release() method at the end of the game:

```
// Create an event system object
FMOD::EventSystem* eventSystem;
FMOD::EventSystem_Create(&eventSystem);

// Initialize the event system and load the project
eventSystem->init(100, FMOD_INIT_NORMAL, 0, FMOD_EVENT_INIT_NORMAL);
eventSystem->load("project.fev", 0, 0);

// Update event system every frame
eventSystem->update();

// Release event system when we are done
eventSystem->release();
```

In order to play an event, we must get a reference to it, by using the fully qualified name of the event, which contains the project name, the name of the event group that contains the event, and the name of the event itself. Then, we can simply use the start() method to play the event:

```
// Get a reference to the event
FMOD::Event* event;
eventSystem->getEvent("ProjectName/EventGroupName/EventName",
                      FMOD_EVENT_DEFAULT, &event);
// Begin playing the event
event->start();
```

Finally, if there is a parameter that we want to modify, we can get a reference to it using the getParameter() method of the event object, and change the value using the setValue() method of the parameter object:

```
// Get a reference to the parameter
FMOD::EventParameter* parameter;
event->getParameter("ParameterName", &parameter);

// Change the value of the parameter
parameter->setValue(2.0f);
```

Summary

In this chapter, we have seen how a sound can be a lot more than just an audio file, how FMOD has a high-level tool called the FMOD Designer, how we can create simple and multi-track sound events in the FMOD Designer, how we can also apply some of these concepts to music and play sound events created in the FMOD Designer from our applications.

6
Low-level Audio

We have now reached the final chapter of this book. So far, we have worked with audio at many different levels of complexity and abstraction, using both low-level and high-level audio engines. These audio engines provide an invaluable help to the developers, and we should definitely use them whenever possible. With their help, we have loaded and played audio files, learnt how to control sound parameters, simulated sound in 3D environments, and created complex, multi-layered, interactive sounds.

In this chapter, however, we will pretend that these audio engines do not exist, and work with nothing more than the bits and bytes that represent sound in a computer. We will then re-implement, in a simplified form, many of the features that FMOD takes care for us. We will also take a brief look at sound synthesis, which is the act of generating sound using mathematical formulas, instead of relying on recorded audio.

The purpose of this chapter is to further our understanding of how sound works, and to gain some insight into many of the features that audio engines implement for us. It should also serve as a starting point for those who are looking to implement complex audio features in their games.

Representing audio data

In *Chapter 1*, *Audio Concepts*, we discussed the most important concepts of digital audio theory. In particular, we saw that a simple array of numbers could represent an audio signal, and talked about topics such as PCM, sampling rate, bit depth, and multi-channel audio.

In this chapter, we will be putting all of those concepts into practice, so make sure you understand them before continuing. For starters, let us look into the meaning of audio data, both in theory and in code.

Audio data is nothing more than a sequence of numbers that represent the amplitude of a sound wave at even time intervals. However, there are many ways to represent numbers on a computer, depending on the amount of memory used to represent them, whether they should be able to store negative numbers, and whether the numbers are integers or floating point numbers. These differences result in the multiple data types provided by C++ to store numbers, such as `int`, `short`, `float`, and `double`. It makes sense then, that audio data can also be stored in several formats, depending on the chosen data type.

In this chapter, we will limit ourselves to the most common audio format, which is the signed 16-bit linear PCM format. In this format, every sample is a 16-bit signed integer (a `signed short` in C++) ranging from -32768 at the minimum amplitude, to 32767 at the maximum amplitude. To simplify the notation when dealing with PCM samples and other quantities, we will be using the following aliases:

```
typedef signed short PCM16;
typedef unsigned int U32;
typedef unsigned short U16;
```

After deciding what format to use, we need to create an array to hold all of the audio samples. The size of the array depends directly on the sampling rate of the sound we want to store, its duration in seconds, and the number of channels being used, according to the following formula:

```
count = sampling rate * duration * channels
```

For example, assuming a sampling rate of 44100 Hz, we could create an array to store exactly 1 second of mono audio data like the following:

```
// 1 second of audio data at 44100 Hz (Mono)
// count = 44100 Hz * 1 second * 1 channel
PCM16 data[44100];
```

If we wanted to store a stereo signal instead, we would need to store twice that amount of information (and the same idea applies to higher amounts of channels). Remember that the most common way to represent stereo audio data is to interleave samples, left and right, in the same array:

```
// 1 second of audio data at 44100 Hz (Stereo)
// data[0] = left, data[1] = right, data[2] = left, etc.
// count = 44100 Hz * 1 second * 2 channels
PCM16 data[88200];
```

Playing audio data

We need a way to submit the audio data to the sound card, so that we can hear the resulting sound. We could use a very low-level audio API, such as PortAudio, which provides the bare minimum functionality required to communicate with an audio device. However, FMOD is also perfectly capable of handling this task, and since we have been using it so far, there is little benefit in changing to a different API now. Therefore, we will use FMOD once again, but only as bridge between the application and the hardware, and our code will handle all of the processing.

The way FMOD allows us to play user created audio data is by first creating a sound with the FMOD_OPENUSER flag, and specifying a callback function that will provide the audio data to the sound.

We must create and fill a FMOD_CREATESOUNDEXINFO structure with a few details regarding the audio data that we will be submitting, such as the sampling rate, format, and number of channels, as well as a pointer to the function that will provide the data itself.

For all of our examples, we will work with a sampling rate of 44100 Hz, use the 16-bit PCM format, and have two channels (stereo). Read the comments for more information about each attribute:

```
// Create and initialize a sound info structure
FMOD_CREATESOUNDEXINFO info;
memset(&info, 0, sizeof(FMOD_CREATESOUNDEXINFO));
info.cbsize = sizeof(FMOD_CREATESOUNDEXINFO);

// Specify sampling rate, format, and number of channels to use
// In this case, 44100 Hz, signed 16-bit PCM, Stereo
info.defaultfrequency = 44100;
info.format = FMOD_SOUND_FORMAT_PCM16;
info.numchannels = 2;

// Size of the entire sound in bytes. Since the sound will be
// looping, it does not need to be too long. In this example
// we will be using the equivalent of a 5 seconds sound.
// i.e. sampleRate * channels * bytesPerSample * durationInSeconds
info.length = 44100 * 2 * sizeof(signed short) * 5;

// Number of samples we will be submitting at a time
// A smaller value results in less latency between operations
// but if it is too small we get problems in the sound
// In this case we will aim for a latency of 100ms
// i.e. sampleRate * durationInSeconds = 44100 * 0.1 = 4410
```

```
info.decodebuffersize = 4410;

// Specify the callback function that will provide the audio data
info.pcmreadcallback = WriteSoundData;
```

Next, we create a looping, streaming sound, specifying the FMOD_OPENUSER mode, and passing it the sound info structure to the third parameter of createStream(). We can then begin playing the sound as normal:

```
// Create a looping stream with FMOD_OPENUSER and the info we filled
FMOD::Sound* sound;
FMOD_MODE mode = FMOD_LOOP_NORMAL | FMOD_OPENUSER;
system->createStream(0, mode, &info, &sound);
system->playSound(FMOD_CHANNEL_FREE, sound, false, 0);
```

As long as the sound is playing, the audio engine invokes our callback function periodically to get the data it requires. The callback function must follow a certain signature that takes three parameters, a reference to the sound object that we created, an array for us to write the audio data into, and the total number of bytes that we should write to the data array. It should also return FMOD_OK at the end.

The data array is defined by a pointer to void (void*) because, as we discussed earlier, there are many different formats for the data to be in. It is up to us to cast the data array to the correct format. Since we created the sound with FMOD_SOUND_FORMAT_PCM16, we have to cast the data array to a signed short* first.

Another important detail is that the length parameter specifies the amount of data to write to the array in bytes, but each of our samples is a signed short, which occupy 2 bytes each. Therefore, we should make sure to write no more than length/2 samples to the data array.

Here is an example of a callback function, which outputs silence by filling the entire audio buffer with zeros. Not very interesting, but it should serve as a good starting point:

```
FMOD_RESULT F_CALLBACK
WriteSoundData(FMOD_SOUND* sound, void* data, unsigned int length) {
  // Cast data pointer to the appropriate format (in this case PCM16)
  PCM16* pcmData = (PCM16*)data;

  // Calculate how many samples can fit in the data array
  // In this case, since each sample has 2 bytes, we divide
  // length by 2
  int pcmDataCount = length / 2;

  // Output 0 in every sample
```

```
    for(int i = 0; i < pcmDataCount; ++i) {
      pcmData[i] = 0;
    }

    return FMOD_OK;
  }
```

Loading a sound

The most common way to get audio data is to read it from an audio file. However, as we have seen before, there are many different audio file formats, and reading the audio data out of them is usually a non-trivial task. This is particularly true with compressed audio file formats, which require decoding the audio data using some algorithm, before we can use it in our application. In general, it is usually better to use an audio engine, or an external library, to read the contents of an audio file.

For educational purposes, we will be reading the audio data from a WAV file. We will, however, work under the assumption that the WAV file we read from is in the canonical form (that is, it contains only a format and a data subchunk, in that order) and that the audio data is stored without any compression. Under these conditions, we know where all of the data is stored, and can simply index into the file to read it. That is certainly not the case for every WAV file, which would require a more complex loading sequence.

The WAV file format builds upon the more generic RIFF file format. A RIFF file is divided into chunks of data. Every chunk begins with a 4-character ASCII identifier, and a 32-bit integer describing how much data is stored in the chunk. Next, there is the actual data of the chunk, which varies depending on the type of the chunk.

All WAV files contain at least the following three chunks (with two of them considered subchunks of the first):

- A **RIFF** chunk containing the string literal: WAVE
- A **Format** subchunk containing information about the audio file
- A **Data** subchunk containing the actual audio data

The following figure shows the contents of a WAV file in a canonical format. Note that if the file contains compressed data, the format subchunk can contain more data than the one shown in the following figure. It is also possible for other chunks to appear in the file, or in a different order:

	Content	Type	Size	Offset
Riff Chunk ID	"RIFF"	char[4]	4	0
Riff Chunk Size	4	u 32	4	4
Format	"WAVE"	char[4]	4	8
Format Chunk ID	"fmt"	char[4]	4	12
Format Chunk Size	16	u 32	4	16
Audio Format	1 for PCM	u 16	2	20
Number of Channels	e.g. 1 or 2	u 16	2	22
Sampling Rate	e.g. 44100	u 32	4	24
Bytes Per Second		u 32	4	28
Bytes Per Block		u 16	2	32
Bits Per Sample	e.g. 16	u 16	2	34
Data Chunk ID	"data"	char[4]	4	36
Data Chunk Size	n	u 32	4	40
Audio Data	n samples	byte[n]	n	44

Now that we have a table listing the contents of a canonical WAV file, let us create a class to load and store all of the information that we care about from the file (that is, the sampling rate, bit depth, number of channels, and the audio data).

Keeping in line with what we used previously in FMOD, we will name this class MySound. For simplicity, every member of the class has public accessibility, although we could provide a few accessor methods instead, while making the data private:

```
class MySound {
 public:
  MySound(const char* path);
  ~MySound();

  U32 samplingRate;
  U16 numChannels;
  U16 bitsPerSample;
  PCM16* data;
  U32 count;
};
```

On the constructor, we open the audio file and read all of the relevant data into the member variables. Note that there is no error checking anywhere, and that this will only work under the conditions described earlier:

```
#include <iostream>
#include <fstream>

MySound::MySound(const char* path) {
    // Open file stream for input as binary
    std::ifstream file(path, std::ios::in | std::ios::binary);

    // Read number of channels and sample rate
    file.seekg(22);
    file.read((char*)&numChannels, 2);
    file.read((char*)&samplingRate, 4);

    // Read bits per sample
    file.seekg(34);
    file.read((char*)&bitsPerSample, 2);

    // Read size of data in bytes
    U32 length;
    file.seekg(40);
    file.read((char*)&length, 4);

    // Allocate array to hold all the data as PCM samples
    count = length / 2;
    data = new PCM16[count];

    // Read PCM data
    file.read((char*)data, length);
}
```

The destructor takes care of cleaning up the memory allocated in the constructor to hold the audio data:

```
MySound::~MySound() {
    delete[] data;
}
```

Playing a sound

Now that we have all of the audio data stored in memory, we are ready to begin playing the sound. In order to do so we must essentially take each of the values stored in the data array, and send them in order to the audio card (in our case, using the callback method that we created earlier).

If the format, sampling rate, and number of channels in the audio data are the same as the output, then this process is as simple as copying values from one array to another. However, the process becomes significantly more complicated if they differ in any way, in particular:

- If our audio data has a different sampling rate from the output, we need to resample the data so that it matches the sampling rate of the output, or the sound will play at a different rate than we expect. This operation is not trivial, and is beyond the scope of this chapter.

- If our audio data is in a different format from the output, we need to convert the data to the new format first. For example, we may need to convert a 32-bit floating point sample into a signed 16-bit integer sample. This is not that complicated, and mostly requires scaling numbers from one range to another.

- If our audio data has different number of channels from the output, we have to adapt the signal to the new number of channels. Adapting a mono signal to a stereo is easy, as we simply need to send a duplicate of the data to both channels. Adapting a stereo signal to mono usually involves adding the values of both channels together, and dividing the result by two.

For the sake of keeping our examples simple, we will assume that the audio data has a very specific format, so that no conversions need to take place:

- It has a sampling rate of 44100 Hz, the same as the output

- It is stored in the PCM16 audio format, the same as the output

- It only has one channel (mono) of data, although the output has two channels (stereo), so that we can see an example of how to implement panning

Under these conditions, we only need two things to play the sound, we need to be able to access the audio data, and we need a variable to keep a track of the current position within the sound (that is, how many samples we have written so far) so that we know which sample to write next. Once the position becomes larger than the number of samples in the data, it means that the sound has finished playing, and we interrupt the process.

Like we did with the sound class, let us also create a class to encapsulate all of the data and behaviors related to playing sounds, which we will name `MyChannel`:

```
class MyChannel {
 public:
  MyChannel() : sound(0), position(0) {}
  void Play(MySound* mySound);
  void Stop();
  void WriteSoundData(PCM16* data, int count);

 private:
  MySound* sound;
  int position;
};
```

Like the channels in FMOD, we should be able to reuse a single channel object for different sounds. Therefore, instead of taking a sound object in the constructor, we only assign the sound object inside the `Play()` method. This method also resets the position value:

```
void MyChannel::Play(MySound* mySound) {
  sound = mySound;
  position = 0;
}
```

The `Stop()` method, on the other hand, simply clears the reference to the sound object:

```
void MyChannel::Stop() {
  sound = 0;
}
```

Finally, the most important portion of the process occurs inside the `WriteSoundData()` method, which will be called from within the audio callback. This method takes two parameters, the array of PCM samples to write to and the size of this array. Notice that this method already expects the `data` array to be in the correct format, instead of the `void*` provided to the audio callback. The `count` also refers to the number of samples in the array, not the number of bytes. There are comments in the code explaining what each line is doing:

```
void MyChannel::WriteSoundData(PCM16* data, int count) {
  // If there is no sound assigned to the channel do nothing
  if(sound == 0) return;

  // We need to write "count" samples to the "data" array
  // Since output is stereo it is easier to advance in pairs
```

```
    for (int i = 0; i < count; i += 2) {

      // If we have reached the end of the sound, stop and return
      if(position >= sound->count) {
        Stop();
        return;
      }

      // Read value from the sound data at the current position
      PCM16 value = sound->data[position];

      // Write value to both the left and right channels
      data[i] = value;
      data[i+1] = value;

      // Advance the position by one sample
      ++position;
    }
  }
```

Using this class, our audio callback becomes a lot simpler, as we can delegate most of the work to the `WriteSoundData()` method of the channel. In the following example there is a single channel object, so we can only play one sound at a time, but later we will see how easy it is to add support for multiple sounds, as well as several other features:

```
MyChannel channel;

FMOD_RESULT F_CALLBACK
WriteSoundData(FMOD_SOUND *sound, void *data, unsigned int length) {
  // Clear output
  memset(data, 0, length);

  // Get data in the correct format and calculate sample count
  PCM16* pcmData = (PCM16*)data;
  int pcmDataCount = length / 2;

  // Tell the channel to write to the output
  channel.WriteSoundData(pcmData, pcmDataCount);

  return FMOD_OK;
}
```

Notice that in the preceding example, we begin by clearing the audio buffer with `memset`. This is necessary because we will not be filling the output with values once the sound stops playing, and FMOD does not clear the buffer automatically between callback calls.

Playing a sound with this architecture is as simple as instantiating the sound, and asking the channel object to play it:

```
MySound* sound = new MySound("explosion.wav");
channel.Play(sound);
```

Pausing a sound

Now that we have the basic functionality for playing sounds implemented using the `MySound` and `MyChannel` classes, we can begin adding more features to it. We will start with the simplest of all, pausing the sound.

We must add a member variable to hold the pause state, and some methods to modify it. We must also remember to initialize this value to `false` inside the constructor, and inside the `Play()` method:

```
public:
  bool GetPaused() const { return paused; }
  void SetPaused(bool value) { paused = value }
private:
  bool paused;
```

Next, all we have to do is add a very simple condition at the beginning of the `WriteSoundData()` method so that it does nothing when the sound is paused. That is as simple as it gets!

```
void MyChannel::WriteSoundData(PCM16* data, int count) {
  if(sound == 0 || paused) return;
  for (int i = 0; i < count; i += 2) {
    if(position >= sound->count) {
      Stop();
      return;
    }
    PCM16 value = sound->data[position];
    data[i] = value;
    data[i+1] = value;
    ++position;
  }
}
```

Looping a sound

The next feature that we will implement is the ability to endlessly make a sound loop. Like the ability to pause a sound, this is also quite trivial to implement. We begin by repeating everything that we did for pausing, but for looping instead:

```
public:
  bool GetLoop() const { return loop; }
  void SetLoop(bool value) { loop = value }
private:
  bool loop;
```

Inside the `WriteSoundData()` method, in the part where we used to detect if the sound had already reached the end, we first check if the loop variable is set to `true`, and if that is the case, we set the position back to the beginning instead of stopping the sound:

```
void MyChannel::WriteSoundData(PCM16* data, int count) {
  if(sound == 0 || paused) return;
  for (int i = 0; i < count; i += 2) {
    if(position >= sound->count) {
      if(loop) {
        position = 0;
      } else {
        Stop();
        return;
      }
    }
    PCM16 value = sound->data[position];
    data[i] = value;
    data[i+1] = value;
    ++position;
  }
}
```

Changing volume

The next few features that we will implement involve modifying the values that are sent to the output. Changing the volume of a sound is probably the simplest of them, as it only requires a multiplication.

Let us start by creating a variable and some methods to control the volume. The volume will be stored as a floating point number between 0 (silence) and 1 (full volume). The SetVolume() method makes sure that the value is always inside this range. We should also reset the volume to 1 whenever a sound begins playing:

```
public:
  float GetVolume() const { return volume; }
  void SetVolume(float value) {
    if(value < 0.0f) volume = 0.0f;
    else if(value > 1.0f) volume = 1.0f;
    else volume = value;
  }
private:
  float volume;
```

In order to play the sound at this volume, all we have to do is multiply each of the original values in the audio data by the value of the volume variable, before we write them to the output. Because the volume variable is a floating point number, we need to cast the result back to PCM16 after the multiplication:

```
void MyChannel::WriteSoundData(PCM16* data, int count) {
  if(sound == 0 || paused) return;
  for (int i = 0; i < count; i += 2) {
    if(position >= sound->count) {
      if(loop) {
        position = 0;
      } else {
        Stop();
        return;
      }
    }
    PCM16 value = (PCM16)(sound->data[position] * volume);
    data[i] = value;
    data[i+1] = value;
    ++position;
  }
}
```

Changing pitch

Changing the pitch of a sound is slightly more complicated than changing its volume. The most basic way to modify the pitch of a sound (although the speed of the sound is also affected) is to control how fast we advance the position value.

So far, we have used a `position` variable that was an integer, and incremented its value by a full unit every time. In order to provide pitch control, we will change that variable to a floating point number, and add a `pitch` variable that determines how much to increment the position.

By default, the `pitch` variable will have a value of 1, which plays the sound at the normal pitch. A value of 2 will double the frequency of the sound, making it sound one octave higher, and a value of 0.5 will halve the frequency of the sound, making it sound one octave lower. For practical reasons, we will limit its value to the range between 0.25 (two octaves below the original sound) and 4 (two octaves above the original sound):

```
public:
  float GetPitch() const { return pitch; }
  void SetPitch(float value) {
    if(value < 0.25f) pitch = 0.25f;
    else if(value > 4.0f) pitch = 4.0f;
    else pitch = value;
  }
private:
  float position;
  float pitch;
```

Inside our `WriteSoundData()` method, we increment the position variable by the pitch amount. The hardest part in the process is how to convert the `position` variable that is now a floating point number, back into an array index. The simplest solution is to use a simple cast, which truncates the value to an integer, and that is what we will use:

```
void MyChannel::WriteSoundData(PCM16* data, int count) {
  if(sound == 0 || paused) return;
  for (int i = 0; i < count; i += 2) {
    if(position >= sound->count) {
      if(loop) {
        position = 0;
      } else {
        Stop();
        return;
      }
```

```
    }
    PCM16 value = (PCM16)(sound->data[(int)position] * volume);
    data[i] = value;
    data[i+1] = value;
    position += pitch;
  }
}
```

However, the truncation from the cast can introduce distortion into the signal. For example, if the position is advancing at a slower pace than normal, it will have many values that are between whole numbers, but because of the truncation from the cast, we will get the same value written multiple times to the output, instead of a flowing sound wave.

A better approach is to use linear interpolation (or another type of interpolation) to calculate a value for the sample that takes the surrounding values and the fractional portion of the position into consideration. For example, using linear interpolation, if the position was 2.25, instead of outputting the value of data[2], we would output a mix of 75 percent of the value of data[2] with 25 percent of the value of data[3] instead.

Changing panning

There are many different approaches to implement stereo panning of a sound. In this section, we will cover a simple approach that works just by modifying the volumes of the left and right channels independently.

Before actually doing any calculations, let us prepare the class for panning by adding two private variables, leftGain and rightGain, to store the volumes of each channel:

```
private:
  float leftGain;
  float rightGain;
```

Then, inside the WriteSoundData() method, we can apply these gains to the data before writing it to the output, just as we did for the volume before. Naturally, we should only apply the values of leftGain and rightGain to their respective channels. In addition, because we need to cast to PCM16 after applying the gains, there is no need to keep the cast from earlier:

```
void MyChannel::WriteSoundData(PCM16* data, int count) {
  if(sound == 0 || paused) return;
  for (int i = 0; i < count; i += 2) {
    if(position >= sound->count) {
```

```
            if(loop) {
              position = 0;
            } else {
              Stop();
              return;
            }
          }
        }
        float value = sound->data[(int)position] * volume;
        data[i] = (PCM16)(value * leftGain);
        data[i+1] = (PCM16)(value * rightGain);
        position += pitch;
      }
    }
```

With these out of the way, we now need to create a floating point variable called pan and some methods to modify it. The pan variable should take values between -1 (full left) and 1 (full right). Whenever the value of pan changes, we call the private UpdatePan() method to calculate new values for leftGain and rightGain:

```
public:
    float GetPan() const { return pan; }
    void SetPan(float value) {
      if(value < -1.0f) pan = -1.0f;
      else if(value > 1.0f) pan = 1.0f;
      else pan = value;
      UpdatePan();
    }
private:
    void UpdatePan();
    float pan;
```

All that is left is to write the UpdatePan() method. There are a few different formulas to calculate the gain values for stereo panning. One of the simplest approaches is to use linear panning, where each channel starts at 0 percent volume in one side, and increases linearly to 100 percent on the other side, while being at 50 percent in the middle. Here is an implementation of linear panning:

```
// Linear panning
void MyChannel::UpdatePan() {
  float position = pan * 0.5f;
  leftGain = 0.5f - position;
  rightGain = position + 0.5f;
}
```

Another approach, which usually yields a smoother transition when panning, is to use **constant-power panning**, where the volume of each channel follows a circular curve, with the volume of each channel being roughly 71 percent in the middle. We have already discussed constant-power panning before, since it is the type of panning used by FMOD for panning mono sounds. Without going into details about the math involved, here is an implementation of constant-power panning:

```
#include <math.h>

#define PI_4 0.78539816339        // PI/4
#define SQRT2_2 0.70710678118     // SQRT(2)/2

// Constant-power panning
void MyChannel::UpdatePan() {
  double angle = pan * PI_4;
  leftGain = (float)(SQRT2_2 * (cos(angle) - sin(angle)));
  rightGain = (float)(SQRT2_2 * (cos(angle) + sin(angle)));
}
```

Mixing multiple sounds

So far, we have only been playing one sound at a time, but it is quite easy to extend what we are doing to play multiple sounds at once. The act of combining multiple sounds into a single output is known as **audio mixing**, and it can be implemented by adding all the audio signals together, and clamping the result to the available range. Looking at our WriteSoundData() method, all we need to do is change the lines of code that write to the data array, so that the samples are added to the existing values, instead of completely replacing them:

```
void MyChannel::WriteSoundData(PCM16* data, int count) {
  if(sound == 0 || paused) return;
  for (int i = 0; i < count; i += 2) {
    if(position >= sound->count) {
      if(loop) {
        position = 0;
      } else {
        Stop();
        return;
      }
    }
    float value = sound->data[(int)position] * volume;
    data[i] = (PCM16)(value * leftGain + data[i]);
    data[i+1] = (PCM16)(value * rightGain + data[i+1]);
    position += pitch;
  }
}
```

In our main application, instead of having a single channel instance, we can now create multiple instances, and call `WriteSoundData()` on all of them:

```cpp
std::vector<MyChannel> channels;

FMOD_RESULT F_CALLBACK
WriteSoundData(FMOD_SOUND *sound, void *data, unsigned int length) {
  // Clear output
  memset(data, 0, length);

  // Get data in the correct format and calculate sample count
  PCM16* pcmData = (PCM16*)data;
  int pcmDataCount = length / 2;

  // Tell every channel to write to the output
  for(int i = 0; i < channels.size(); ++i)
    channels[i].WriteSoundData(pcmData, pcmDataCount);

  return FMOD_OK;
}
```

Implementing a delay effect

We have already discussed, back in *Chapter 4, 3D Audio*, that DSP effects are algorithms that modify the audio data to achieve a certain goal. Now we will see an example of how to implement a simple delay effect. The way a basic delay effect works, is to keep a separate buffer of data, and store the audio data that has already played in it. The size of the buffer determines how long it takes between the original sound and its echo plays. Then, we simply need to mix the audio data that is playing, with a portion of the old signal that was stored in the buffer, which produces a delay. Let us examine the following `MyDelay` class definition, which encapsulates the effect:

```cpp
class MyDelay {
public:
  MyDelay(float time, float decay);
  ~MyDelay();
  void WriteSoundData(PCM16* data, int count);

private:
  PCM16* buffer;
  int size;
  int position;
  float decay;
};
```

The `MyDelay` class constructor takes two parameters, `time` and `decay`. The first parameter controls how many seconds it takes between the sound and the first echo occurs. The second parameter controls how much energy is lost during each echo.

The class stores a buffer of PCM16 samples, which we initialize in the constructor so that it can store the equivalent of `time` seconds of data at a sampling rate of 44100 Hz. This buffer starts completely filled with zeros. It also contains a `position` variable that will be used to cycle through the buffer:

```
MyDelay::MyDelay(float time, float decay) : position(0), decay(decay)
{
  size = (int)(time * 44100);
  buffer = new PCM16[size];
  memset(buffer, 0, size * 2);
}
```

The destructor deletes all the data allocated in the constructor:

```
MyDelay::~MyDelay() {
  delete[] buffer;
}
```

Finally, the `WriteSoundData()` method does all of the work. It begins by taking each sample in the output, and mixing it with a portion of the sample stored in the buffer at the current position. Next, we take this new value and write it back to the output, as well as to the buffer. Finally, we increment the position variable to the next sample, wrapping around the end of the buffer:

```
void MyDelay::WriteSoundData(PCM16* data, int count) {
  for (int i = 0; i < count; ++i) {
    // Mix sample with the one stored in the buffer at position
    data[i] = (PCM16)(data[i] + buffer[position] * decay);

    // Record this new value in the buffer at position
    buffer[position] = data[i];

    // Increment buffer position wrapping around
    ++position;
    if(position >= size)
      position = 0;
  }
}
```

To test this effect out, simply create an instance of it in the main application, and call the `WriteSoundData()` method at the end of the audio callback:

```
// When the application starts
MyDelay* delay = new MyDelay(1.0f, 0.50f);

// Inside the audio callback
for(int i = 0; i < channels.size(); ++i)
   channels[i].WriteSoundData(pcmData, pcmDataCount);
delay->WriteSoundData(pcmData, pcmDataCount);
```

Synthesizing a sound

Before we end this chapter, it is also worth realizing that not every sound needs to come from an audio file. It is also possible to generate sounds from scratch, using only mathematical formulas. We call this process, **sound synthesis**, and there are entire books just about this subject.

Certain sound waves are particularly common in sound synthesis because of how easy they are to calculate. We have already talked about one of these sound waves before, the sine wave. Other common examples are the square wave, the sawtooth wave, and the triangle wave, all represented in the following figure:

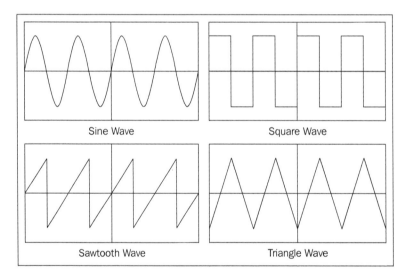

Sine Wave   Square Wave

Sawtooth Wave   Triangle Wave

We will now see how to synthesize each of these sound waves, by creating a class `MyOscillator`. The use case for this class is pretty much the same as the `MyDelay` class described earlier; just create an instance of it, and call the `WriteSoundData()` method from the audio callback to make it play:

```
#include <math.h>
#define PI 3.14159265359
#define TWO_PI 6.28318530718

class MyOscillator {
 public:
  MyOscillator();
  void SetVolume(double value) { volume = value; }
  void SetFrequency(double frequency);
  void WriteSoundData(PCM16* data, int count);

 private:
  double phase;
  double increment;
  double volume;
};
```

The class contains three member variables, `phase`, which describes how far we are along the sound wave, `increment`, which depends on the frequency of the sound and describes how much we should advance the phase between each sample, and `volume`, which can be changed through the `SetVolume()` method. Note that we are using doubles for everything instead of floats, as sound synthesis tends to require more precision in its calculations.

All that the class constructor does is initialize the phase to zero, the volume to one, and set the increment by calling `SetFrequency()` with a default value of 440 Hz:

```
MyOscillator::MyOscillator() : phase(0.0), volume(0.5) {
  SetFrequency(440.0);
}
```

The `SetFrequency()` method calculates the correct increment value using the following formula. In this case, we have hardcoded the sampling rate to be 44100 Hz, but there could be a parameter to control the sampling rate:

```
void MyOscillator::SetFrequency(double frequency) {
  increment = frequency / 44100.0 * TWO_PI;
}
```

As usual, most of the work is handled inside the WriteSoundData() method. First, we calculate the value of the sound wave for the current phase, and scale it into the correct range for a PCM16 sample (by multiplying by 32767, which is the highest number that can be stored in a signed short). Next, we write this result to the audio output, mixing it with anything that was already there. Finally, we increment the phase, and wrap it so that it always stays within the 0 to 2 PI range:

```
void WriteSoundData(PCM16* data, int count) {
  for(int i = 0; i < count; i += 2) {
    // Calculate sample value
    double value = sine_wave(phase) * 32767.0 * volume;

    // Mix sample with output
    data[i] = (PCM16)(data[i] + value);
    data[i+1] = (PCM16)(data[i+1] + value);

    // Increment phase
    phase += increment;

    // Wrap phase to the 0-2PI range
    if(phase >= TWO_PI)
      phase -= TWO_PI;
  }
}
```

The actual audio data is generated by the sine_wave() method highlighted in the previous code. All that this method does is call the standard sin() function on the phase value and return the result. We can easily swap this method with any of the following implementations, depending on the type of sound wave that we want to play:

```
double sine_wave(double phase) {
  return sin(phase);
}

double square_wave(double phase) {
  return phase <= PI ? 1.0 : -1.0;
}

double downward_sawtooth_wave(double phase) {
  return 1.0 - 2.0 * (phase / TWO_PI);
}
double upward_sawtooth_wave(double phase) {
  return 2.0 * (phase / TWO_PI) - 1.0;
}
```

```
double triangle_wave(double phase) {
  double result = upward_sawtooth_wave(phase);
  if(result < 0.0)
    result = -result;
  return 2.0 * (result - 0.5);
}
```

Summary

In this chapter, we have seen how to work directly with the bits and bytes of audio data, how to load the audio data from a canonical WAV file, how to play and control audio data using only low-level operations, how to implement a simple delay effect, and how to synthesize some basic sound waves.

Index

audio source direction
  setting 44
audio source position
  setting 43, 44
audio source range
  setting 44
audio sources
  about 42
  creating 43
audio source velocity
  setting 43, 44
audio system
  creating 15
  managing 15

B

breaking glass sound effect
  creating 61

C

car engine
  sound, simulating 66
ChangeSemitone() method 35
channel groups
  controlling 31
channel handle 25
channels
  grouping 30
chorus effect 50
chunks, WAV files
  Data subchunk 77
  Format subchunk 77
  RIFF 77
complex ambient track, of forest
  creating 67
compressor effect 50
constant-power panning 89
Core Audio 13
createChannelGroup() method 30
createDSPByType method 51
createSound() method 16
createStream() method 16
cues 56

D

Data subchunk 77
default ambient reverb
  setting 48
delay effect 50
  implementing 90, 91
digital signal processing. *See* DSP effect
digital signals 9
DirectSound 13
distortion effect 50
Doppler effect 41
DSP effect 50, 90
DSP effect, types
  chorus 50
  compressor 50
  delay 50
  distortion 50
  echo 50
  flanger 50
  high-pass filter 50
  low-pass filter 50
  noise removal 50
  normalize 50
  parametric EQ 50
  pitch shift 50

E

echo effect 50
effects, FMOD
  about 51
  simple radio effect 52
  time stretching 51

F

façade design pattern 19
FLAC 12
flanger effect 50
FMOD
  about 13, 75
  advantages 14
  effects 51
  obstruction, simulating 49
  occlusion, simulating 49
  positional audio 43

Thank you for buying
Getting Started with C++ Audio Programming for Game Development

About Packt Publishing

Packt, pronounced 'packed', published its first book *"Mastering phpMyAdmin for Effective MySQL Management"* in April 2004 and subsequently continued to specialize in publishing highly focused books on specific technologies and solutions.

Our books and publications share the experiences of your fellow IT professionals in adapting and customizing today's systems, applications, and frameworks. Our solution based books give you the knowledge and power to customize the software and technologies you're using to get the job done. Packt books are more specific and less general than the IT books you have seen in the past. Our unique business model allows us to bring you more focused information, giving you more of what you need to know, and less of what you don't.

Packt is a modern, yet unique publishing company, which focuses on producing quality, cutting-edge books for communities of developers, administrators, and newbies alike. For more information, please visit our website: www.packtpub.com.

Writing for Packt

We welcome all inquiries from people who are interested in authoring. Book proposals should be sent to author@packtpub.com. If your book idea is still at an early stage and you would like to discuss it first before writing a formal book proposal, contact us; one of our commissioning editors will get in touch with you.

We're not just looking for published authors; if you have strong technical skills but no writing experience, our experienced editors can help you develop a writing career, or simply get some additional reward for your expertise.

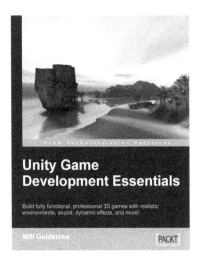

Unity Game Development Essentials

ISBN: 978-1-84719-818-1   Paperback: 316 pages

Build fully functional, professional 3D games with realistic environments, sound, dynamic effects, and more!

1. Kick start game development, and build ready-to-play 3D games with ease

2. Understand key concepts in game design including scripting, physics, instantiation, particle effects, and more

3. Test & optimize your game to perfection with essential tips-and-tricks

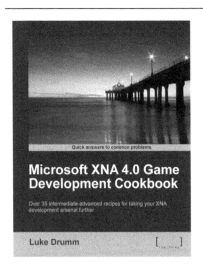

Microsoft XNA 4.0 Game Development Cookbook

ISBN: 978-1-84969-198-7   Paperback: 356 pages

Over 35 intermediate-advanced recipes for taking your XNA development arsenal further

1. Accelerate your XNA learning with a myriad of tips and tricks to solve your everyday problems

2. Get to grips with adding special effects, virtual atmospheres and computer controlled characters with this book and e-book

3. A fast-paced cookbook packed with screenshots to illustrate each advanced step by step task

Please check **www.PacktPub.com** for information on our titles

AndEngine for Android Game Development Cookbook

ISBN: 978-1-84951-898-7   Paperback: 380 pages

Over 70 highly effective recipes with real-world examples to get to grips with the powerful capabilities of AndEngine and GLES 2

1. Step by step detailed instructions and information on a number of AndEngine functions, including illustrations and diagrams for added support and results

2. Learn all about the various aspects of AndEngine with prime and practical examples, useful for bringing your ideas to life

3. Improve the performance of past and future game projects with a collection of useful optimization tips

CryENGINE 3 Cookbook

ISBN: 978-1-84969-106-2   Paperback: 324 pages

Over 90 recipes written by Crytek developers for creating third-generation real-time games

1. Begin developing your AAA game or simulation by harnessing the power of the award winning CryENGINE3

2. Create entire game worlds using the powerful CryENGINE 3 Sandbox.

3. Create your very own customized content for use within the CryENGINE3 with the multiple creation recipes in this book

www.ingramcontent.com/pod-product-compliance
Lightning Source LLC
LaVergne TN
LVHW080100070326
832902LV00014B/2344